DESIGN TECHNOLOGY
INTERNATIONAL BACCALAUREATE

MAYANK RAJ SINGH

Copyright © Mayank Raj Singh
All Rights Reserved.

This book has been published with all efforts taken to make the material error-free after the consent of the author. However, the author and the publisher do not assume and hereby disclaim any liability to any party for any loss, damage, or disruption caused by errors or omissions, whether such errors or omissions result from negligence, accident, or any other cause.

While every effort has been made to avoid any mistake or omission, this publication is being sold on the condition and understanding that neither the author nor the publishers or printers would be liable in any manner to any person by reason of any mistake or omission in this publication or for any action taken or omitted to be taken or advice rendered or accepted on the basis of this work. For any defect in printing or binding the publishers will be liable only to replace the defective copy by another copy of this work then available.

I dedicate this book to the IBDP Design Technology students. All the best for your IBDP journey!

Contents

CHAPTER ONE

Human Factors & Ergonomics

1.1 Product Design

Product design is the process of developing a usable product that meets customers' needs by defining the users' problems and finding creative solutions for these problems. The term is also used to refer to the result of this process, the design qualities of an existing product. Product design is based on design thinking, an approach for creatively solving problems.

Figure 1.1 Product Design

We can define the following 3 characteristics to describe product design:

Product design is a complex process that includes a variety of tasks, ranging from research to prototyping and testing.

Product design is human-centred (as all the good things are), but involves more consideration of the needs of the business and market situation.

Product design is never-ending (or almost so). You cannot say it is a clearly defined set of steps. Everyone follows the structure they consider the most suitable and efficient, but the process may include an unexpected number of iterations that are crucial for understanding the problem and finding the best solution to it.

Now, let's dive into details and start with the core processes that lie at the heart of product design.

Main processes in product design

Product designers take care of the project during its whole product lifecycle: from initial research to concept creation to prototyping and usability testing.

This section will briefly explain a set of concepts that form the foundation of modern product design.

Product discovery

When it comes to making product decisions, we always have doubts about whether our solution will succeed or fail. Product discovery lowers the risks associated with the feasibility of our ideas.

In a nutshell, product discovery is a process to fine-tune your ideas by learning what your customers' true needs and problems are and then deciding on the best strategy to solve them.

The goal of product discovery is to quickly define whether the idea is good or bad and answer the following questions:

1. Will customers be willing to buy the product?

2. Will the product be easy to use for our customers?

3. Will engineers be able to implement our ideas?

4. Will stakeholders support our ideas?

To answer these questions, you have to carefully examine the market and potential users. Here are some design methods that help us during the product design process.

1.2 Ergonomics

Ergonomics (or human factors) is the scientific discipline concerned with the understanding of interactions among humans and other elements of a system, and the profession that applies theory, principles, data and methods to design to optimize human well-being and overall system performance.

The word ergonomics comes from the Greek word "ergon" which means work and "nomos" which means laws. It's essentially the "laws of work" or "science of work". A good ergonomic design removes incompatibilities between the work and the worker and creates the optimal work environment.

Ergonomics draws on many disciplines to optimize the interaction between the work environment and the worker.

1. Disciplines

2. Anthropometry

3. Biomechanics

4. Mechanical engineering

5. Industrial engineering

6. Industrial design

7. Information design

8. Kinesiology

9. Physiology

10. Psychology

Ergonomics Domains of Specialization

According to the International Ergonomics Association, there are three broad domains of ergonomics: physical, cognitive, and organizational.

Physical Ergonomics

Physical ergonomics is concerned with human anatomical, anthropometric, physiological and biomechanical characteristics as they relate to physical activity.

This is the ergonomics domain we are most concerned with in the workplace, and most of the content on this site is very much focused on workplace ergonomics.

Workplace Ergonomics

The science of fitting workplace conditions and job demands to the capabilities of the working population. Ergonomics is an approach or solution to deal with several problems—among them are work-related musculoskeletal disorders.

At its core, workplace ergonomics is really about building a better workplace. When jobs are designed to match the capabilities of people, it results in better work being produced and a better experience for the person doing it.

Through that lens, ergonomics creates value on several fronts. It's good for your people and good for your business.

Benefits of Ergonomics :

Lower costs

Higher productivity

Better product quality

Improved employee engagement

Better safety culture

The ergonomics improvement process systematically identifies ergonomic hazards and puts in place engineering and administrative control measures to quantifiably reduce risk factors.

Ergonomics Process

Assess Risk: Conducting an ergonomic assessment is a foundational element of the ergonomics process. Your ergonomic improvement efforts will never get off the ground without being able to effectively assess jobs in your workplace for the musculoskeletal disorder (MSD) risk factors.

Plan Improvements: The core goal of the ergonomics process is to make changes to your workplace that reduce risk. Making changes at scale requires a significant planning effort that includes prioritizing jobs to be improved, identifying effective improvement ideas, and cost-justifying the improvement projects.

Measure Progress: Measurement is an important component of any successful continuous improvement process. High-performing ergonomics programs are constantly measured using both leading and lagging indicators.

Scale Solutions: By establishing a common set of tools to train your workforce, assess risk, plan improvements, measure progress, and design new work processes, you'll be able to scale ergonomics best practices throughout your organization.

Cognitive Ergonomics

Cognitive ergonomics is concerned with mental processes, such as perception, memory, reasoning, and motor response, as they affect interactions among humans and other elements of a system.

Relevant topics :

mental workload

decision-making

skilled performance

human-computer interaction

human reliability

work stress

training as these may relate to human-system design

Organizational Ergonomics

Organizational ergonomics is concerned with the optimization of sociotechnical systems, including their organizational structures, policies, and processes.

Relevant topics :

communication

crew resource management

work design

design of working times

teamwork

participatory design
community ergonomics
cooperative work
new work paradigms
virtual organizations
telework
quality management
Ergonomics Applications

The applications of ergonomics are everywhere and many books are written on the subject, so I won't try to cover them all in specific detail here.

But consider this.

The definition of work is an "activity involving mental or physical effort done to achieve a purpose or result."

That sounds like just about everything we do, and when you consider that ergonomics is about designing the work environment to optimize human well-being and overall system performance, you begin to realize that ergonomics plays a major factor in our lives – at work, at home and all the places in between.

1.3 Anthropometrics

Design is human-centred; therefore, designers need to ensure that the products they design are the right size for the user and therefore comfortable to use. Designers have access to data and drawings, which state measurements of human beings of all ages and sizes. Designers need to consider how users will interact with the product or service. Use and misuse are important considerations.

Anthropometric data sets can vary significantly between populations. Particularly in the fashion industry, the variance in these data sets impacts the size range of clothes for particular markets.

Anthropometric Data

Term: The aspect of ergonomics that deals with body measurements, particularly those of size, strength and physical capacity.

Term: Static (structural) data – Human body measurements when the subject is still.

The measurements when the body is in a fixed position, i.e static, such as height. joint to joint, skin and bulk.

Data is collected using standardised equipment such as callipers, stadiometers or anthropometers.

Design contexts include chair height, door width, etc

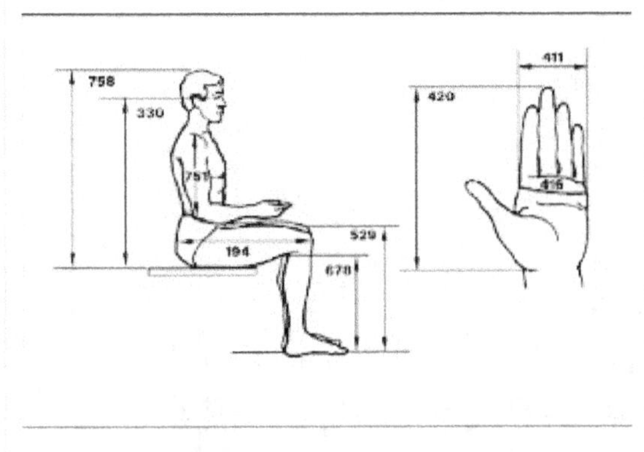
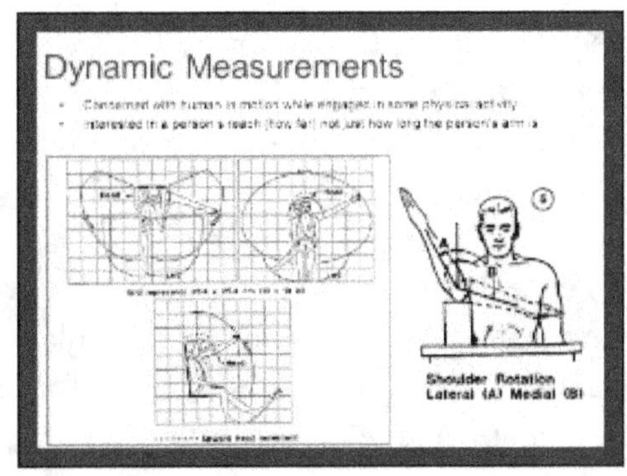

Static Data

Dynamic Data

Can opener – requires the dynamic data of grip and torque.

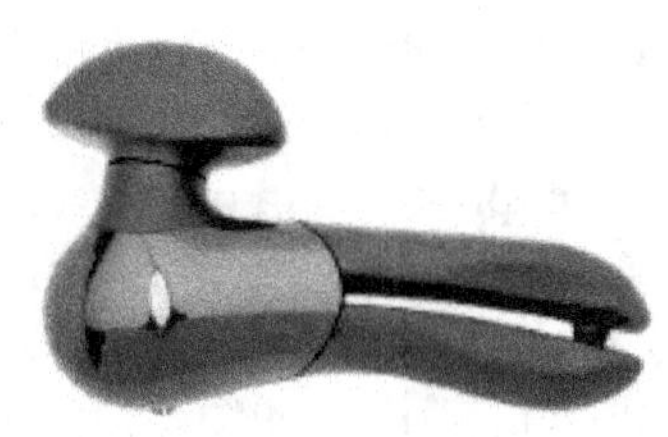

Butterfly Can Opener – can be hard to use for some people.

Ergonomically designed – big easy grip handles and wing nut.

Fig 1.2 Anthropometric Data

Term: Dynamic (functional) data – Human body measurements are taken when the subject is in motion related to the range and reach of various body movements. E.g. crawling height, overhead reach and the range of upper body movements.

The measurements that relate a range or reach of various types of body movements such as reach, grip strength, reaction times, etc

Carrying out a task.

Design contexts in can openers, car console features, book shelving reach, etc

Static Data Dynamic Data

Can opener – requires the dynamic data of grip and torque.

Butterfly Can Opener – can be hard to use for some people. Ergonomically designed – big easy grip handles and wing nut.

Activity: On the Padlet match 1 dynamic and 1 static data with a design context.

Primary Data versus Secondary Data

Term: Primary data: Data collected by a user for a specific purpose.

It is collected by the researcher or designers themselves. This would be carried out if there is a specialised group of people that may not have been studied.

Term: Secondary data: Data collected by someone other than the user.

There is a great deal of anthropometric data available.

It is collected and stored in databases or books.

Website of a collection of sources.

Reliability and limitations of collecting anthropometric data.

Age, gender, ethnicity, etc need to be considered.

Body shape and sizes can change over time.

Percentiles and Percentile Ranges

Term: Percentile range: That proportion of a population with a dimension at or less than a given value.

You need to be able to interpret percentile tables for user populations in a design context.

a). Consider the 5th, 50th and 95th percentiles in particular, and percentile ranges such as 2.5th to 97.5th and 5th to 95th.

b). In the table (Male Rowers) below the lightest (least heavy) rowers are the 5th percentile and they weigh 69.8 kgs or less.

c). Ergonomic4schools' Anthropometry section has a nice table showing design contexts. Take note of when dynamic or static data is used.

d). Interpret percentile tables based on different national and international populations, gender and age. Personal City U on diversity.

e). When considering percentile ranges the design context factors in as well.

f). If comfort or safety is important, a range of percentiles must be considered. For example, motorcycle helmets need to fit snugly to function properly in protecting the head.

g). If a product is in short use and safety or comfort such as a school desk or waiting room seating, then the 50th percentile would be appropriate.

h). Interpret percentile tables to calculate dimensions related to a product.

Activity: From the table below:

1. Identify the sitting height of the 50th percentile.

2. Which is the longest arm length and which group do they belong to?

Table 3 *Anthropometric profile chart for male junior rowers (n=383)*

Body dimension	Percentiles						
	5	10	25	50	75	90	95
Body mass (kg)	68.8	73.0	77.2	81.9	87.0	92.3	94.7
Stature (cm)	177.3	179.2	183.6	187.6	191.4	195.2	196.6
Sitting height (cm)	91.5	93.7	94.5	96.7	98.9	100.8	102.3
Leg length (cm)	84.4	85.3	88.1	90.8	93.3	95.0	97.3
Arm length (cm)	77.7	78.5	80.8	83.0	85.2	87.0	88.4
Biacromial diameter (cm)	38.6	39.4	40.4	41.5	42.5	43.5	44.2
Biiliocristal diameter (cm)	27.9	28.4	29.3	30.2	31.1	32.2	33.0
Humerus width (cm)	7.1	7.2	7.4	7.6	7.8	8.0	8.2
Femur width (cm)	9.6	9.8	10.0	10.3	10.6	11.0	11.1
Biceps girth (cm)	29.7	30.5	31.6	33.1	34.3	35.3	35.8
Upper arm girth (cm)	26.6	27.3	28.5	30.0	31.2	32.1	32.8
Forearm girth (cm)	26.3	27.0	27.6	28.5	29.5	30.3	30.7
Thigh girth (cm)	52.7	53.8	55.5	58.0	60.2	62.0	63.4
Calf girth (cm)	34.4	35.3	36.6	37.8	39.0	40.0	40.7
Biceps skinfold (mm)	2.7	3.0	3.2	3.6	4.4	5.3	5.9
Triceps skinfold (mm)	5.0	5.3	6.3	7.7	9.4	10.7	12.1
Subscap. skinfold (mm)	6.6	7.1	7.8	8.3	9.6	10.9	11.5
Suprailiac skinfold (mm)	4.3	4.6	5.1	6.1	7.6	9.5	10.5
Thigh skinfold (mm)	6.3	7.1	8.7	10.9	13.6	16.1	18.0
Calf skinfold (mm)	4.8	5.3	6.3	7.8	9.9	12.5	14.2

Percentiles Table of Rowers

Percentile Range Curve

Fig 1.3 Percentiles Table of Rowers & Percentile Range Curve

Clearance, Reach and Adjustability

Term: Clearance: The physical space between two objects.

eg: two people in a doorway or the space between sitting people.

Term: Reach: A range that a person can stretch to touch or grasp an object from a specified position.

eg arm extension or work envelope.

Term: Adjustability: The ability of a product to be changed in size, commonly used to increase the range of percentiles that a product is appropriate for.

Car driver seats have many adjustments that can accommodate many people, eg seat height, distance to the sterling wheel, and even height of the steering wheel.

Often adjustability is used in design contexts where a range of sizes is not possible or expensive to produce.

Adjustability Reach Clearance

Range of sizes versus Adjustability

Term: Range of sizes: A selection of sizes a product is made in that caters for the majority of a market.

a. Clothes or motorcycle helmets come in a range of sizes to accommodate as many percentiles ranges.

b. This is often done for comfort and safety. If something is not comfortable then it can lead to unsafe situations due to fatigue.

Term: Adjustability: see above.

Bike Sizes and Adjustability

Bicycles use a combination of a range of sizes (to suit different heights) as well as adjustability (the seat and handlebars).

Consider how products can be adaptable for different markets or adjustable to cater for most.

International-Mindedness

A wide selection of anthropometric data is published and regionalized, for example, Asian data versus western European data. The designer must work with data appropriate to the target market.

Theory of Knowledge

Do the methods of data collection used in design technology have more in common with disciplines in the human sciences or the natural sciences?

1.4 Psychological Factors

Human beings vary psychologically in complex ways. Any attempt by designers to classify people into groups merely results in a statement of broad principles that may or may not be relevant to the individual. Design permeates every aspect of human experience and data pertaining to what cannot be seen such as touch, taste, and smell are often expressions of opinion rather than checkable fact.

The analysis of the human information processing system requires a designer to critically analyse a range of causes and effects to identify where a potential breakdown could occur and the effect it may have.

Psychological Factor Data

Term: Human factor data related to psychological interpretations caused by light, smell, sound, taste, temperature and texture.

These factors can better help understand and optimise the user's safety, health, comfort and performance.

These are a significant part of ergonomics and human efficiency, comfort and safety can be affected by these factors.

Methods of Collecting Psychological Factor Data

Data Collection through 4 types of measurement data scales, which include; nominal, ordinal, interval and ratio.

Qualitative versus Quantitative Data

Term: Qualitative Data – Typically descriptive data is used to find out in-depth the way people think or feel – their perception. Useful for research at the individual or small (focus) group level.

a. Nominal or Ordinal Scale (Qualitative) – taste, smell, temperature and texture.

b. Qualitative data may be used in a design context relating to psychological factors, but individuals vary in their reaction to the data.

c. For example, one person will find a room temperature comfortable while another person will find it uncomfortable, though the temperature is constant.

Term: Quantitative Data – Data that can be measured and recorded using numbers. Examples include height, shoe size, and fingernail length.

a. Interval or Ratio Scale (Quantitative) – sound, temperature and light.

Human Information Processing Systems

Term: Human information processing system – An automatic system that a person uses to interpret information and react. It is normally comprised of inputs, processes (which can be sensory, central and motor), and outputs.

Can be represented using a flow chart.

a. Below is a flow diagram; the arrows represent the flow of information through the system.

b. The boxes represent functional elements in the processing chain, where information is processed.

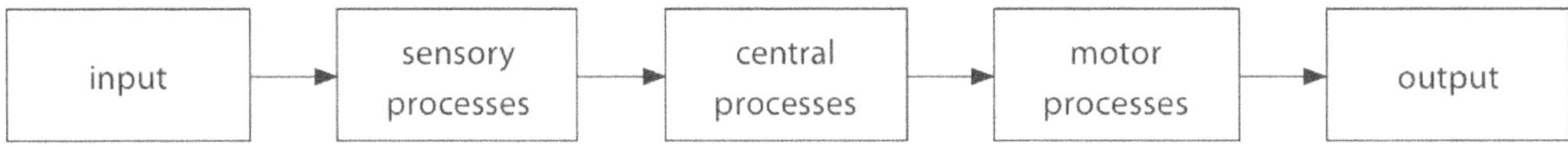

Fig 1.4 Flow chart (provided by IB)

Scenario 1: Where we can apply the human information processing system to a common task, such as a finger in hot water.

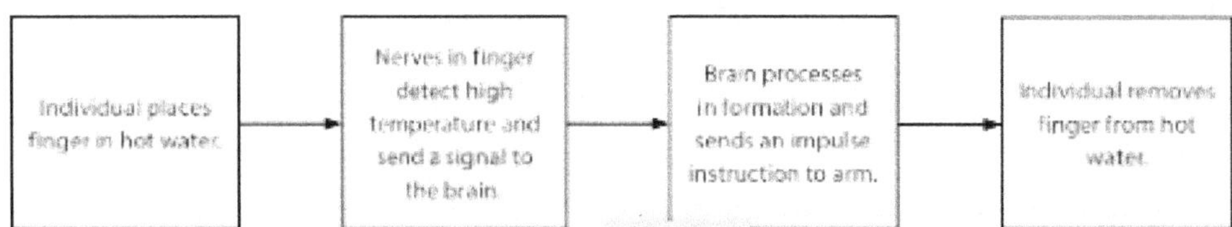

Fig 1.5 Scenario 1

Scenario 2: when using a mobile phone to make a telephone call.

a. The input would be the number to be called.

b. The sensory processes would be the eyes, which would transmit information to the brain.

c. The brain is the central processing unit, which examines the information and selects a response coded as a series of nerve impulses transmitted to the hand and muscles.

d. These are the motor processes, which reconvert the instructions into actions, that is, outputs.

Activity:

You are driving a car and you see a red traffic light up ahead. Develop a flow chart that represents the human information processing system that would occur.

A Breakdown in the Human Information Processing System (Effects and Reasons)

What happens if the information processing system breaks down?

In the car activity above you would have (hopefully) concluded that the output would be the foot pressing the brake so the car will stop. If there is a breakdown in the human information processing system then a car crash is a likely event.

Here a few things could have occurred such as

a. Slow reaction time (between seeing the red light and reacting). Stimulus/input as not seen (Red light or car/pedestrian in the intersection). Response/output was not done/slipped/foot got caught, etc.

b. In other words,

The information inputs may be incompatible with the sensory receptors.

At the central processing stage, the incoming information may be incorrect or no suitable responses to it are available.

The motor output stage may be unable to perform the actions specified by the central processing unit.

Some reasons include:

a. Age – too young and maybe have not learnt the skills (long term memory), too old maybe forget what to do, or too weak to carry out the task.

b. Strength – too weak to carry out the task

c. Skills – do not have the necessary skills yet, may have forgotten the skills, skills needed are too complex

d. Health – when mental or physical health is comprised which may lead to not carrying out the necessary tasks.

e. Environmental factors – see below for more details.

Effect of Environmental Factors

Term: Environmental factors – A set of psychological factors that can affect the performance of an individual that comes from the environment that the individual is situated.

a. Environmental factors include sound, temperature, lighting, air quality (pollutants) and smell.

b. Environmental factors can affect different individuals in different ways. Individuals react differently to sensory stimuli.

c. Efficiency and comfort are affected by such factors.

d. It becomes important to optimize environmental factors to maximize workplace performance.

e. This can be challenging as user responses to environmental factors are different, some people will find 22C perfect while for others it may too cold! ... though the temperature is constant.

Fig 1.6 Hot n' Cold

Perception: The way in which something is regarded, understood or interpreted.

a. The users respond differently to different environmental factors.

b. Perception has an impact on the accuracy and reliability of psychological factors data

c. Quantitative data may be used in a design context relating to psychological factors, but individuals vary in their reaction to the data.

d. For cxample, one person will find a room temperature comfortable while another person will find it uncomfortable,

e. How warm or cold work environments can affect the performance of an individual.

f. Thermal comfort describes a person's psychological state of mind and involves a range of environmental factors: air temperature, the heat radiating from the Sun, fires and other heat sources, air velocity (still air makes people feel stuffy, moving air increases heat loss), humidity, and personal factors (clothing and metabolic rate).

g. Hopefully in an office environment where a number of people work together, the thermal environment satisfies the majority of the people.

h. Thermal comfort is not measured by air temperature (quantitative), but by the number of people complaining (qualitative) of thermal discomfort.

Activity:

a. The above temperature example can guide you for this activity.

b. Show how users respond differently to each of the following, sound, lighting, air quality and smell.

c. Put your answers on the class Padlet.

Alertness

Alertness: The level of vigilance, readiness or caution of an individual.

Environmental factors induce different levels of alertness.

a. Temperature: too warm and you get sleepy and less alert – too cold and you become more alert. Next time you are on a long-haul flight note the temperature fluctuations while flying.

b. Sound: too loud which can be distracting or even cause harm, high pitched or repetitive on/off noises also become distracting.

c. Lighting: too dim hard to see things need to get close or strains the eyes, natural versus fluorescent (can affect people's eyes)

d. Air quality: excess dust or other pollutants could cause people to find it hard to breathe, maybe a cough, etc. Certain essential or aroma oils are said to improve alertness

e. Smell – bad smells (whew) will draw one's attention away as opposed to the smell of a hot apple pie.

International Mindedness

The origin of psychology (as a mainly western academic subject) along with recent neurological insights on a global scale need to be taken into account in applying any psychological factors to global design problems.

Theory of Knowledge

How might the collection and interpretation of data be affected by the limitations of our sense perception?

1.5 Physiological Factors

Designers study physical characteristics to optimize the user's safety, health, comfort and performance.

Understanding complex biomechanics and designing products to enable full functionality of body parts can return independence and personal and social well-being to an individual.

Physiological factor data

Types of physiological factor data available to designers:

- For example, bodily tolerances such as fatigue and comfort.
- muscle strength in different body positions
- endurance in different body positions
- visual acuity
- tolerance to extremes of temperature
- the frequency range of human hearing,
- size
- eye/hand coordination etc

How physiological factor data are collected:

using a wide range of methods, such as performance testing, user trials and observations, collection of anthropometric data, etc.

Comfort and fatigue

When users interact with products, they may put stress on their bodies which leads to comfort and fatigue. The data designers collect related to comfort and fatigue in form design decisions, such as jar openers for the elderly or people with Arthritis.

Fatigue: When people are put under physical or mental stress/activities for extended periods, fatigue can set in. People react differently when they are fatigued. Errors can creep in which then could prove dangerous. Designers need to understand people's tolerances and design products and environments that help to reduce fatigue.

Comfort: This varies between people. For instance, the type of bed that a person will choose is determined by the firmness of the mattress.

Biomechanics

Biomechanics is the research and analysis of the mechanics of living organisms.

The importance of biomechanics to the design of different products considering muscle strength, age of the user, user interface (surface texture, handle size, etc) and torque.

In a kitchen: viewing distances, pulling strength, lifting strength and turning strength.

In a can opener, valve wheel, corkscrew, door handle, jam jar lid – torque becomes important.

International Mindedness

It is important that the physiological factor data are either regional/national data or that great care is taken when applying data from one source to a potentially inappropriate target market.

Theory of Knowledge

This topic is about human factors. How do ethical limitations affect the sort of investigations that can take place where human subjects are involved?

CHAPTER TWO

Resource Management & Sustainable Production

2.1 RESOURCES AND RESERVES

As non-renewable resources run out, designers need to develop innovative solutions to meet basic human needs for energy, food and raw materials. The development of renewable and sustainable resources is one of the major challenges of the 21st century for designers.

Much of the development of new resources is the product of creating sustainable solutions to existing problems.

The legacy of the industrial revolution is now being felt as we face resource depletion. The challenge for designers is to continue to develop products that meet the needs of humans while conserving the environment for future generations.

Renewable and Non-Renewable Resources

Renewable resource

Term: A natural resource that can replenish with time or does not abate at all

These include biofuels solar, wind, hydro, wave, tidal, thermal and biofuels

A natural resource qualifies as a renewable resource if it is replenished by natural processes at a rate almost the same as its rate of consumption by humans or other users.

Renewability

Term: This term refers to a resource that is inexhaustible and therefore can be replenished quick enough.

Hardwood trees (such as many rainforest species) take a fair bit of time to mature to a point where it useable as a resource, therefore, it is considered non-renewable. On the other hand, softwoods (such as pines or conifers) mature more quickly and are considered a renewablelelelele resource.

Renewable vs Non-renewable

Non-renewable resources

Term: A natural resource that does not replenish at a sustainable rate; a source that will run out if the rate of extraction is maintained.

These include fossil fuels such as natural gas, oil, coal, gasohol and nuclear energy

These resources are very useful sources of energy. This energy is needed to manufacture products and provide power to businesses, factories and homes.

The bad aspect about this is that these resources are running out and the human dependency on them is very high.

Reserves

Term: A natural resource that has been identified in terms of quantity and quality.

A proven reserve is those resources that can be economically and technically extracted.

Reserves exist but they might not be viable at this moment such as gold in seawater

Rare Earth Mineral Reserves

Oil Reserves

Economic and Political Importance

The extraction of oil has been at the centre of many issues removing resource security and international treaties. Students need to understand the issues/impact surrounding resourresourceity for Nations/Governments and international treaties.

Governments need to balance the economic benefits and political impact (including social aspects) of resource extraction.

The Invasion of Kuwait in 1990 is one such example. Iraq was accusing the Kuwait government of 'slant drilling' from the border into Iraqi reserves thus stealing Iraqi oil. It is also thought to be that Iraq invaded to procure Kuwaiti oil which was considered to be 20% of the global reserves. A third reason was that Kuwait was overproducing oil thwhichdroppedthe price of global oil which affect the Iraqi economy.

Often, multinational companies licensed to extract resources have limited consideration for the local population.

Oil companies are often brought into the country to explore possible new fields and then develop them. The oil companies pay the government a set amount which can develop wealth. This can produce local employment and other opportunities.

Rare earth minerals/elements which are highly desired/needed and valuable came with a set of issues. The countries that have them can receive a financial windfall, and local communities gain skilled employment, however, the environmental impon for local communities is damaging. An article from the TheGuardian.

The economic and political importance of material and land resources and reserves considering:

set-up costs – typically are high and perhaps national/local governments cannot afford to set up the infrastructure and the extraction site so outside multinationals could be invited.

the efficiency of conversion –

sustainable and constant supply –

social impact – can bring jobs (skilled and unskilled) and wealth, employment could be permanent or temporary (short-term excavation/extraction),

environmental impact – as mentioned above

decommissioning – is economically quite expensive, especially with nuclear reactors

International Mindedness

The impact of multinational companies when obtaining resources in different countries/ regions can be a significant issue for the local population and have major social, ethical and environmental implications.

Theory of Knowledge

To what extent should potential damage to the environment limit our pursuit of knowledge?

2.2 WASTE MITIGATION STRATEGIES

The abundance of resources and raw materials in the industrial age led to the development of a throwaway society, and as resources run out, the many facets of sustainability become a more important focus for designers. The result of the throwaway society is large amounts of materials found in landfill, which can be considered a new source to ones from.

The exploration of possible solutions to eliminate waste in our society has given rise to ideas developed as part of the circular economy. By redesigning products and processes, the waste from one product can become the raw material of another.

Throwaway then and now

Strategies to Mitigate Waste

Re-use

Term: This is reusing a product in the same context or a different context.

Reusing is utilising an object more than one time.

This takes into account conventional reuse where the object is used again for a similar purpose and new-life reuse where it is used for an innovative purpose.

An example of reusing is using disposable plastic or glass bottles to drink water from over again.

Reusing car tyres

Minion from car tyres on bored panda

Paper reuse into furniture

Recycle

Term: Recycling refers to using the materials from obsolete products to create other products.

Recycling consists of processing used materials into novel products to avert squandering potentially functional materials.

It decreases the consumption of unsullied raw resources, trims down energy usage, lowers air and water pollution by dropping the need for "usual" waste discarding, and lastly lolowersreenhouse gas emissions.

An example of recycling is recycled paper.

Recycled Toilet Paper

Recycling bins

Repair

Term: Is the reconstruction or renewal of any part of an existing structure or device.

Repair Manifesto

Wristwatch repair

Recondition

Term: Reconditioning is rebuilding a product so that it is in an "as new" condition, by repairing it, cleaning it, or replacing parts.

Contexts include car engines, tyres or refurbished electronics.

Re-engineer

Term: A re-engineered product has been significantly redesigned, with improved engineering, from its original form.

In may: use raw materials that were meant for another product or manufacturing process, use environmentally friendly materials, recycle some of the original components and improve performance.

The Dyson Ball Vacuum cleaner has been re-engineered. The vacuum still functions in collecting dust but the method of doing it is different. They redesigned the suction system.

Re-engineered Dyson Vacuum Cleaner (follow Link)

Pollution & Waste

From Wikipedia "Pollution is the introduction of contaminants into the natural environment that cause adverse change.[1] Pollution can take the form of chemical substances or energy, such as noise, heat or light. Pollutants, the components of pollution, can be either foreign substances/energies or naturally occurring contaminants.

Landfill in Poland

From Wikipedia, Wastes are unwanted or unusable materials. Waste is any substance which is discarded after primary use, or it is worthless, defective and of no use.

Something to ponder? – This is subjective as one person's idea of waste may whereas another person may find it useful!

Smokey Mountain in the Philippines

Zabbaleen of Mokkattam in Cairo

Methodologies for Waste Reduction and Designing out Waste

Dematerialization

Term: The reduction of total material and energy throughput of any product and service.

Dematerialization of a Toothbrush

Dematerialization improves production efficiency by saving, reusing or recycling materials, components and products.

It impacts every stage of the product life cycle: material extraction; eco-design; cleaner production; environmentally conscious consumption patterns; recycling of waste.

It may mean smaller, lighter products and packaging; the replacement of physical products with virtual products (email instead of paper, web pages instead of brochures); home working, and so on.

Reduction of total material and energy throughput of a product or service, and the limitation of its environmental impact through reduction of raw materials at the production stage; energy and material inputs at the user stage; waste at the disposal stage

There are potential results of successful dematerialization.

Product Recovery Strategies at End of Life/Disposal

Term: The processes of separating the parts of a product to recover the parts and materials.

Use and recovery of standard parts at the end of product life.

Recovery of raw materials.

Take back the legislation.

Trade-in.

Recycling bins/locations.

Employ a circular economy.

Circular Economy

Term: An economy model in which resources remain in use for as long as possible, from which maximum value is extracted while in use, and the products and materials are recovered and regenerated at the end of the product life cycle.

An economic model that closed loop system where the materials/resources are in constant use. At the end of the product life cycle the mat,erial waste (or obsolete product material) is recycled/recovered.

The material waste is a resource in the system and is regenerated at the end of the product life cycle.

A circular economy requires designers to consider the subsequent use of materials, components and the embedded/embodied energy in a product.

This can only be achieved by innovative design and consideration of further cycles of development.

Designers must ask themselves the question, "How can this product be made to be made again?"

There are three central strands to this concept:

cradle-to-cradle (Topic 2.6) design thinking which looks at the whole design and manufacturing process.

design for disassembly (Topic 4.5) which allows for the recovery of materials and components.

design inspired by nature that favours diversity and in which there is no waste (biomimicry).

Innovative design techniques might include:

the use of smart (shape) memory screws,

dissolvable circuit boards and adhesives (glue),

the use of clips rather than adhesives or screws,

biological materials (such as bioplastics) that can be safely returned to the biosphere with no toxic dyes or other materials.

Equally important are the systems in which the product moves: How will the materials or components be recovered and made use of again?

The designer and manufacturer need to consider this when developing products.

One way forward is to develop different business models where users buy performance through leasing rather than purchasing. This offers interesting job opportunities in creating reverse supply chains as well as engaging design challenges and opportunities.

Splosh – A company has a set where a customer purchases a one-off starter kit and then fills the bottle with a sachet of cleaning liquid and rm water and they are all ready to go.

Adding water reduces packing (reduction of materials) and weight (important for transportation – reduction is fuel)

Saves on materials, energy and waste.

If the bottle is reused 20 times it means 95% less packaging waste

The linear and circular models of the economy from the Ellen MacArthur Foundation

The above models show the traditional linear, where the material is extracted, manufactured and diseased in a landfill. The circular model – one of them the bio-waste is returned to enrich the earth. In the left model, the technical waste is recycled and rescued in the continued production.

Ellen MacArthur Foundation of Circular economy includes overview, diagrams and case studies.

Final Word: Designing out waste and designing for closed-loop recycling will be more important as resources become scarcer and waste becomes more expensive. Therefore, developing products for product recovery and dematerialization will become an essential element of innovation.

International Mindedness

The export of highly toxic waste from one country to another is an issue for all stakeholders.

Theory of Knowledge

The circular economy can be seen as an example of a paradigm shift in design. Does knowledge develop through paradigm shifts in all areas of knowledge?

2.3 ENERGY UTILIZATION, STORAGE AND DISTRIBUTION

Efficient energy use is an important consideration for designers in today's society. Energy conservation and efficient energy use are pivotal in our impact on the environment. A designer's goal is to reduce the amount of energy required to provide products or services using newer technologies or creative implementation of systems to reduce usage. For example, driving less is an example of energy conservation, while driving the same amount but with a higher mileage car is energy efficient.

As we develop new electronic products, electrical energy power sources remain an ever-important issue. The ability to concentrate electrical energy into ever-decreasing volume and weight is a challenge for designers of electronic products.

Embodied Energy

Term: Embodied energy – The total energy required to produce a product.

Term: Energy utilization – The method with which energy is used.

Total energy consumed in production (cradle to [factory] gate) and throughout the lifecycle of a product (cradle to grave)

Is the sum of all energy needed to produce a product or service.

It is highly useful to calculate how successful/effective a product or service produces or saves energy.

Embodied energy in a pound of product

The embodied energy of common material

Distributing Energy: National and International Grid Systems

Term: National and international grid systems – An electrical supply distribution network that can be national or international. International grids allow electricity generated in one country to be used in another.

Term: Energy Distribution -The method with which energy is transported from a source to where it is used.

Energy is distributed over national and international grid systems

Egypt's Aswan Dam produces enough electricity that Egypt sells it to Sudan. On the USA and Mexico border, there are three locations where power is sent across the border.

Power nationally distributed is sent for domestic, commercial and industrial use including electric vehicles.

This is a highly centralised grid system.

How a grid works

Asia Pacific Power Grid

Italian National Grid

Power Distribution

Local Combined Heat and Power (CHP)

Term: A system that simultaneously generates heat and electricity from either the combustion of fuel or a solar heat collector.

It is an efficient and clean approach to generating electric power and thermal energy from a single fuel source.

It can either replace or supplement conventional separate heat and power.

Instead of purchasing electricity from the local utility company and burning fuel (oil, gas etc) in an on-site furnace or boiler to produce thermal energy.

This can be taken care of by an industrial or commercial facility that can use CHP to provide both energy services in one energy-efficient step. from the EPA website.

Reduces the negative impact on the environment

Saves the consumer money

Also known as co-generation

CHP and efficiency

Systems for Individual Energy Generation

Term: Individual energy generation is the ability of an individual to use devices to create small amounts of energy to run low-energy products.

is the small-scale generation of heat and electric power by homes (also small businesses and small communities) to meet their own needs.

It is an alternative or can supplement traditional centralized grid-connected power.

Lower negative impact on the environment

Lower costs for the consumer

High initial capital cost

Can sell excess electrical power back to the National Grid

BBC article on Generating, storing and selling in your home.

Also known as micro-generation

House with self-generation

Quantification and Mitigation of Carbon Emissions

Term: Quantification of carbon emissions – Defining numerically the carbon emissions generated by a particular product

Food Carbon Footprint

Global Carbon Footprint

Quantification

record carbon emissions

discover how much is being produced

discover who/ where it is produced

track your carbon footprint

Mitigation

Humans' intervention in the reduction of carbon emissions

These contribute to global warming

Resulting in melting polar caps, rising seas, desertification,

provide 'Sinks' that can reabsorb carbon emissions

A 'Sink' are forests, vegetation or soils.

UN Article on Mitigation

Energy Storage – Batteries, Capacitors and Capacities

Term: Energy Storage –The method with which energy is stored for later use.

A battery is a device consisting of two or more electrochemical cells that convert stored chemical energy into electrical energy (Wikipedia)

The capacitor is an electronic component that temporally stores electrical energy.

Capacity is the amount of electric charge it can deliver (measured in amp-hours)

Batteries have a huge impact on the portability of electronic products –

Through the development of new technologies, batteries have become more efficient and smaller.

First Chemical Battery

Pretty small battery!

Types of Batteries

See the table below with regards to the relative cost, efficiency, environmental impact and reliability of different types of batteries.

Battery TypeRelative CostEfficiencyEnvironmental ImpactReliability

Hydrogen fuel cells High Medium Low

Lithium Medium High Low

NiCad High Medium High

Lead Acid Low LowHigh

LiPo (lithium polymer) High High Low

The environmental impact can be assessed using an environmental impact assessment matrix and life cycle analysis (LCA).

International Mindedness

There are instances of energy sources (for example, oil and electricity) crossing national boundaries through cross-border networks leading to issues of energy security.

Theory of Knowledge

The Sun is the source of all energy and essential for human existence. Is there some knowledge common to all areas of knowledge and ways of knowing?

2.4 CLEAN TECHNOLOGY

Clean technology is found in a broad range of industries, including water, energy, manufacturing, advanced materials and transportation. As our Earth's resources are slowly depleted, demand for energy worldwide should be on every designer's mind when generating products, systems and services. The convergence of environmental, technological, economic and social factors will produce more energy-efficient technologies that will be less reliant on obsolete, polluting technologies.

The legislation (law) for reducing pollution often focuses on the output and, therefore, end-of-pipe technologies. By implementing ideas from the circular economy, pollution is negated and waste eliminated.

Drivers (push) for Cleaning up Manufacturing:

Manufacturers may react to:

Legislation is a driving force for the industry to clean up manufacturing processes.

current or forthcoming legislation (laws)

to conform with government legislation

to avoid penalties

The pressure created by the local community and media

communities have made it known that they don't want harmful (to humans, ecology and the environment) industries

pressure groups such as Greenpeace or even a small community town

this can sometimes force legislation to be developed and enacted

Reasons for cleaning up manufacturing/industry include:

promoting positive impacts

ensuring neutral impact or minimizing negative impacts through conserving natural resources

reducing pollution and use of energy

reducing waste of energy and resources

International Legislation and Targets

International legislation and targets are developed for reducing pollution and waste:

Term: Legislation – Laws considered collectively to address a certain topic.

The role and scale of legislation are dependent upon the type of manufacturing and the varied perspectives in different countries. Legislation (as mentioned above) provides a motivation (perhaps not willingly) for the industry to clean up manufacturing processes.

Manufacturers react to the legislation by cleaning up their act or ignoring it (this happens in some countries as legislation is ibeingibeingibeingibeingnbeing being forced).

Manufacturers don't want to pay to clean up production; this cuts into profits.

International targets, such as those of the Kyoto Protocol in 1997 (see video below), The Copenhagen Accord in 2009, and The Paris Agreement in 2015 are set and agreed upon to reducgreenhouseouse gases to combat global warming.

The difficulties of getting nations to agree to the targets can be for many reasons, such as nationsssss being at different stages of economic and social development, attitudes to the environment, or placing more value on economic gain than the environment.

Legislation is monitored and policed and how it can be promoted for manufacturers.

How legislation can be monitoring and policing

The UN on water

Is it ethical to prevent a developing country from producing high carbon emissions through industrial development when developed countries have been the main generators of carbon emissions through their industrial revolutions and economic development?

China is a current example as it has done in 20 odd years what it took USA and Europe about 100 years.

Incremental and Radical solutions

Incremental solutions

Term: Incremental solutions – Products which are improved and developed over time leading to new versions and generations.

Often, manufacturing processes are improved in terms of efficiency and amount of embodied energy over time.

This incremental development of a manufacturing process can require major refits and the addition of new elements to the manufacturing process.

This allows a company to plan strategically how it will make the changes – this allows for better budget control but requires long-term planning.

the impact is not as drastic as radical solutions.

AdvantagesDisadvantages

Use of existing trusted technologies. Take too long.

No,/limited downtime in production (continued profits)Small changes may not meet the overall legislation requirements.

Less uncertainty of success due to the trusted, known technology.Need to make small changes often.

Can quickly respond to legislation (forthcoming or changing).Saturated (crowded) marketplace/ competition.

Radical solutions

Term: Radical solutions – Where a completely new product is devised by going back to the roots of a problem and thinking about a solution differently.

Radical solutions can make a great and sudden impact;

They can require the replacement of a whole system.

This can be costly and time-consuming where a company may be in down time

AdvantagesDisadvantages

Exploration of new technologies.Costly (both if technology outfitting and loss of profits during downtime).

High potential for market growth.Costly R&D, training and capital (equipment).

Creation of new industries.High uncertainty of success.

Fewer competitors.Possibility of high market resistance.

PateningPatenting new solutions – financial and repetitional benefits. Development is unpredictable incorporating specific starts and stops.

Enhance reputation and be innovative and radical.

End-of-Pipe Technologies

Term: Technology that is used to reduce pollutants and waste at the end of a process.

Technology that is used to reduce pollutants and waste at the end of the industries production processes.

Industries include water, energy, manufacturing, advanced materials and transportation.

An example of this is filters installed on the end of industrial smokestacks.

End-Of-PipeEnd-Of-Pipe vs Clean Production

Trash Traps

Carbon Capture

System Level Solutions

Term: Solutions that are implemented to deal with the whole system, rather than just components.

Is concerned with the prevention of pollutants as a whole – i.e. production system-wide

Often radical implementation

Clean Technology

No Environmental Protection

Articles of interest

Clean Production vs End of Pipe

Clean technology Website from where the images came from

Clean technology and profits

Clean Technology

Term: Products, services or processes that reduce waste and require the minimum amount of non-renewable resources.

"Clean technology includes recycling, renewable energy (wind power, solar power, biomass, hydropower, biofuels, etc.), information technology, green transportation, electric motors, green chemistry, lighting, greywater, and many other appliances that are now more energy efficient. It is a means to create electricity and fuels, with a smaller environmental footprint and minimise pollution. To make green buildings, transport and infrastructure both more energy efficient and environmentally benign" (Wikipedia accessed Jan 19 2016).

Climate Clean Technology

Clean Technology Matrix

Examples of Clean Tech

International Mindedness

The development of clean technology strategies for reducing pollution and waste can positively impact local, national and global environments.

Theory of Knowledge

International targets may be seen to impose the view of a certain culture onto another. Can one group of people know what is best for others?

2.5 GREEN DESIGN

The starting point for many green products is to improve an existing product by redesigning aspects of it to address environmental objectives. The iterative development of these products can be incremental or radical depending on how effectively new technologies can address the environmental objectives. When newer technologies are developed, the product can re-enter the development phase for further improvement.

The purpose of green design is to ensure a sustainable future for all.

Green Design – Cradle to the Grave

Term: Green design is the designing of products to have a reduced environmental impact throughout their life.

Sustainable products provide social and economic benefits while protecting public health, welfare and the environment throughout their life cycle—from the extraction of raw materials to final disposal (cradle to the grave).

Design objectives for green products

Design objectives for green products fall into three categories, materials, energy and pollution/waste.

Materials

Ensuring that the packaging and instructions encourage efficient and environmentally friendly use (this can fall under the pollution category as we ll) materials.

Minimizing the number of different materials used in a product.

Labelling of materials so they can be identified for recycling.

Increasing efficiency in the use of materials and resources.

Energy

Increasing efficiency in the use of energy.

Pollution and waste

Ensuring that the planned life of the product is most appropriate in environmental terms and that the product functions efficiently for its full life.

Analysing and minimizing potential safety hazards (not sure where this goes).

Reducing to a minimum any long-term harm caused by the use of the product.

Reducing or negating environmental damage or pollution from the materials selected.

Reducing or negating noise or smell pollution.

Consider the effects of the disposal of the end of life of the product.

Drivers for green design (consumer pressure and legislation)

Drivers for green design include consumer pressure and legislation, among others.

Consumer Pressure

Term: Collections of individuals who hold a similar viewpoint on a particular topic, for example, the environment, who take action to promote positive change to meet their goals.

The public has become aware of environmental issues through media focus on issues such as the destructive effect of chlorofluorocarbons on the ozone layer; acid rain in Northern European forests and the nuclear accident at Chornobyl

Increased public awareness has put pressure on corporations and governments through voting and purchasing power.

The consumer will seek out products that are energy efficient which will be cheaper to run providing savings for the consumer.

Legislation

Term: Laws considered collectively to address a certain topic.

Environmental legislation has encouraged the design of greener products that tackle specific environmental issues, for example, eliminating the use of certain materials or energy efficiency.

Raised awareness of environmental issues is increasing legislation in many countries. This can lead to financial penalties on companies who do not demonstrate environmental responsibility. Many people will not behave responsibly unless forced to do so, therefore, legislation forces the issue.

Examples of legislation:

Plastic Labelling

One problem with the recycling of plastics is knowing what plastic antigovernment legislation requires laberequiringastic products with the plastic-type plastic-typeinMcDonald'sercome this issue.

CFCs, or chlorofluorocarbons, are harmful greenhouse gases that erode the ozone layer, allowing UV rays to be absorbed and trapped on on on on the Earth and causing global warming. CFCs could be found in Styrofoam, air conditioning coolants, and aerosol cans.

In response (both consumer and government), McDonald's'sin several MEDCs (more economically developed countries) were banned from using Styrofoam containers that contained CFCs and were forced to find alternatives to their old packaging. See news article

Green/High-Performance Building Legislation in the States

Green legislation

Catalytic Converter in Cars

Term: These are laws and regulations that are based on conservation and sustainability principles, followed by designers and manufacturers when creating green products.

Green legislation encourages incremental rather than radical changes:

for example, legislation requiring car manufacturers to install catalytic converters for cars (end-of-pipe technology) tackles the environmental issue of car emissions.

Green legislation is effective as it involves incremental changes (refer to Topic 2.4).

The Designer's Role

The environmental impact of the production, use and disposal of a product can be modified by the designer through careful consideration at the design stage.

In developing the product brief, formulating the product design specification and choosing the material and manufacturing process, the potential environmental impact of the product is assessed with the specific objective of reducing this impact and minimising it over the longer term.

Strategies for green design (incremental and radical)

Most strategies for green design often involve a focus on one or two

Coca-Cola Plant Bottle

environmental objectives when designing or re-designing products. For example bioplastics in place of traditional plastics like in the PlantBottle from Coca-Cola.

There are many other examples of this, such as:

To choose non-toxic, sustainable-produced or recycled materials which don't need as much energy to process.

To manufacture and produce products using less energy.

To produce products that are long-lasting and better functioning so there is less replacement and use of products.

Design products using the concept of being able to recycle them whether done.

Incremental:

Term: Products which are improved and developed over time leading to new versions and generations.

These areas arise are small changes to the design of the product over some time.?

This may include changes in in in in recycled or recyclable materials. Composite materials can be difficult, expensive or can't be recycled.

material optimisation.

limit the number of materials. A tetra pack has multiple layers of materials which, in the past, made it difficult to recycle.

Manufacturing techniques – using clean technology such as end-of-pipe.

Introduce design for disassembly.

Radical:

Term: Where a completely new product is devised by going back to the roots of a problem and thinking about a solution differently.

This may include

making big and courageous whole changes to the design of a product or service.

complete overhaul of the manufacturing process.

using radical clean technology systems

Strategies for designing green products

Most strategies for green design involve focusing on one or two environmental objectives when designing or re-designing a product, for example, the use of recyclable materials.

When evaluating product sustainability consider the following: Raw materials used:

dematerialization.

low environmental impact materials (eg bioplastics, recycled paper, etc).

use of recycled or recyclable materials.

Packaging:

same as above on 'raw materials used.

Reduce incorporation of toxic materials or VOCs:

End-of-life disposal issues:

make it last – reduce obsolescence

enhance recyclability – design for disassembly

Energy in production and use (see next point):

Production methods:

Clean production.

energy efficiency.

Atmospheric pollutants such as VOCsle to implement green design

A reasonable timescale, generally a short 5 years, is implemented for incremental much longer for radical.

This allows for manufacturers to plan and develop design objectives

It is more cost-effective.

Principles Of Environmental Law

The prevention principle

Term: The avoidance or minimization of producing waste about the production, use and disposal of a product.

Actions should be taken before damage occurs.

This is usually based on a past catastrophe or prior scientific data/research.

The precautionary principle

Term: The anticipation of potential problems about the environmental impact of the production, use and disposal of a product.

Actions should be taken so that the risk of damage is avoided.

There may be evidence but perhaps not conclusive) about the risk of environmental harm.

This allows protective measures to be taken without having to wait until the damage materialises.

For example, we know that air pollution can cause respiratory illness but how much air pollution is acceptable?

International Mindedness:

The ability and will of different countries to enact environmental legislation vary greatly.

Theory of Knowledge:

Green issues are an area where experts sometimes disagree. On what basis might we decide between the judgments of experts if they disagree?

2.6 ECO-DESIGN

Consideration of the environmental impact of any product, service or system during its life cycle should be instigated at the earliest stage of design and continue through to disposal. Designers should have a firm understanding of their responsibility to reduce the ecological impact on the planet. Eco-design concepts currently have a great influence on many aspects of design.

The smartphone is an innovative example of converging technologies that combine multiple technologies into one space-saving device. The resultant reduction of materials and energy used in production and distribution has environmental benefits.

Eco-design

Term: A design strategy that focuses on three broad environmental categories – materials, energy, and pollution/waste.

- This makes eco-design more complex and difficult to do.

The Major Considerations of the United Nations Environmental Programme Manual on Eco- design

The UN released a manual on Eco-design in 1996. It outlined major considerations:

- reduce the creation and use of toxic materials
- increase recyclability
- reduce energy consumption
- increase the use of renewable resources
- increase product durability – reducing planned obsolescence
- reduce material requirements for products and services

The emphasis of the guidelines will vary depending on the type of product to be designed and the target market.

The timescale for Implementing Eco-design

- Some factors that can influence the timescale include:
- cost, available technology,
- radical or whole system overhaul,
- eco-design is more complex
- all of which can add to the timescale.

The "cradle to grave" and "cradle to cradle" Philosophy

Term: Cradle to Grave – A design philosophy that considers the environmental effects of a product all of the way from manufacture to disposal.

- It is a key principle of the linear economy.

Term: Cradle to Cradle – A design philosophy that aims to eliminate waste from the production, use and disposal of a product. It centres on products which are made to be made again.

- It is a key principle of the circular economy.
- Made to be made – is when a product is designed it is conceived in such a way that it can be made again using the same/most materials/resources of the original product, once it has been disposed of.
- Cradle to Cradle ® (C2C) is a holistic approach to design popularized by Professor Michael Braungart and William McDonough. Braungart and McDonough offer Cradle to Cradle ®certification to products that measure up to the standards they set.
- According to their website (www.c2ccertified.org): "The target is to develop and design products that are truly suited to a biological or technical metabolism, thereby preventing the recycling of products which were never designed to be recycled in the first place."

Life Cycle Analysis (LCA)

Term: The assessment of the effect a product has on the environment (LCA) through five stages of its life: pre-production; production; distribution (including packaging); utilization; and disposal.

Designers use LCA to assess and balance environmental impact over a product's life cycle.

It can highlight areas with opportunities to reduce the environmental impact.

It makes the designer think about changing product design to reduce the impact such as green or sustainable product designs

LCA stages:

pre-production;

is the obtaining of natural resources;

it can be very polluting (strip-mining) or can have a smaller effect on the environment (shaft mining),

includes transporting the raw material to processing industries

production

is the processing of the resources and shaping etc. to make the product.

Once again it could be damaging to the environment (such as a large factory spewing out smoke) or have a small impact (a carpenter hand crafting children's toys)

distribution including packaging;

includes taking the product from the factory to the warehouse, from the warehouse to the store, and the package.

It could have a large impact (as is the case with an imported object from around the world in a Styrofoam box) or a very low impact (made and sold in the same place with a biodegradable box or no packaging) utilization is about the product's use and the effect that has on the environment.

A diesel generator for example will pollute the air and make noise pollution while a solar panel will make next to none.

disposal

depends on both the product and the method of disposal. Recycling one aluminium can will make fewer environmental problems than throwing one away even if they are identical.

Biodegradable objects can be reused, recycled, or left to be broken down and add nutrients to the soil, depending on the object one or the other would be preferable.

Paper is best recycled because of the chemicals used to make it and the logging of forests to obtain the pulp while a banana peel is completely useless for anything but compost.

Environmental considerations

water and soil pollution

water and soil degradation

air contamination

noise

energy consumption

consumption of natural resources

pollution and effect on ecosystems.

LG's LCA – Click the image for a report

Environmental Impact Assessment Matrix

The LCA matrix is a useful tool for designers of eco-products and systems.

LCA Matrix

Benefits of organizing the life cycle stages and the environmental considerations into an environmental impact assessment matrix in which elements differ in importance according to the particular design context.

It is targeted at particular product categories—products with high environmental impacts in the global marketplace, for example, washing machines and refrigerators.

LCA identifies conflicts that have to be resolved through prioritization.

It is not widely used in practice because

it is difficult, costly and time-consuming.

The complex nature of LCA means that it is not possible for a lone designer to undertake it and a team with a different specialism is required.

LCA is complex, time-consuming and expensive, so the majority of eco-designs are based on less detailed qualitative assessments of likely impacts of a product over its life cycle.

However, in the re-innovation of the design of a product or its manufacture, specific aspects may be changed after considering the design objectives for green products, such as

selecting less toxic materials or using more sustainable sources.

a product may be distributed differently.

its packaging may be redesigned.

minimize the use of packaging.

optimize energy efficiency in use.

design for disassembly.

minimize parts/components.

use recyclable materials.

ENVIRONMENTAL AREA: AIR POLLUTION

ACTIVITYRISK IMPACT RATING (CIRCLE ONE NUMBER IN EACH ROW)

Pre-production: Transport of all materials to factory543210

Production: Manufacturing process waste output543210

Distribution: Transport of product to retailers543210

Distribution: Manufacturing of packaging543210

Utilization: Use of product during working life543210

Disposal: Disassembly and recycling of materials543210

A simple example of an environmental impact assessment matrix – from the IBO

Environmental impact assessment matrices can be infinitely more complex, focusing on one particular stage of LCA at a time and breaking processes down into individual steps, often focusing on output in terms of resources used, wasted and by-products generated and released.

The simplest example is the use of a checklist to guide the design team during a product's design development stages.

The roles and responsibilities of the designer, manufacturer and user at each stage of the product life cycle.

Roles and responsibilities vary between them

The user/consumer has little control in the early stages but more so in the use and disposal of the product.

Similarly, with the designer and manufacturer.

Pre-productionProductionDistributionUtilizationDisposal

DesignerLowMid-HighMid-HighHighHigh

ManufacturerHighHighMidLowLow

UserLowLowLowHighHigh

Activity: Carry out an LCA on a washing machine and refrigerator.

"Design for the Environment" (DfE) software

Term: Software that allows designers to perform Life cycle analysis (LCA) on a product and assess its environmental impact.

Eco-Designer LCA

Design for the Environment description.

There is software available, such as Autodesk Inventor, Eco-designer or Solidworks that allows designers to DfE. They

allow the designer to carry out LCA.

select materials and manufacturing techniques that reduce environmental effects.

run scenarios that can minimize materials.

optimise designs to get cost-effective products that are environmentally concerned.

Product Cycle

Term: Product Cycle – Also known as the product life cycle, it is a cycle that every product goes through from introduction to withdrawal or discontinuation.

Product Life Cycle (a bit dated!)

Product Life Cycle and Marketing

The First Mouse

Where is the computer mouse in the Product Life Cycle? – SMH Link to the article

Four main stages

There are four main stages of the product life cycle which are, introduction, early, mature and late.

During the early stages, the product has just recently been introduced into the market and tends not to sell well and mayyyyyyyyyy bee overpricetoto break-breakeven so undergoes many changes.

During the Mature stages of the product cycle, the product is now reached its peak where little changes to its design occur and sell very well.

During the late stage, the product's sales decline and become obsolete.

Designing is part of the product cycle.

A need is generated and a product is designed, manufactured, and sold.

The product eventuabecomesming obsolete (out of use).

Distributors, retailers, accountants and production engineers, who all affect the cycle, complicate the cycle.

Unlike in the design process, the designer is not necessarily in control of the cycle.

In CAD (computer-aided design) and CAM (computer-aided manufacture), the designer becomes part of the cycle by creating the prototype from a personal computer.

The role of the designer:

Designing is part of the product cycle: as a need is generated, a product is designed, made and sold, eventually becoming obsolete.

The cycle is complicated by distributors, retailers, accountants and production engineers, all of whom influence the cycle. Although the designer is an integral part of the process, he or she is not necessarily in control (unlike in the design process).

Computer-aided design (CAD) and computer-aided manufacture (CAM), where a prototype is produced by the designer from his or her personal computer (PC), blur this distinction.

The role of the manufacturer

In the selection of manufacturing techniques – preferably limiting environmental effect – injection moulding produces very little waste

Quality control – controlling errors and waste

Specify standard components and sub-assemblies

Attempt to minimise: energy usage, emissions, water pollution and other elements of the LCA.

This can be done through the introduction of management systems.

The role of the user

Market pull from consumers

Spending patterns – a need for a durable product versus a disposable one

Disposal of the product

Consumers can force designers and manufacturers to be more green usually through their buying power

Provide feedback to manufacturers

Converging Technologies

Term: The synergistic merging of nanotechnology, biotechnology, information and communication technologies and cognitive science.

Converging Technology

Converging Technology

AdvantagesDisadvantages

A single device with multiple functions

Eliminates the need to buy multiple devices

miniaturization of products increases portability

reduce the need for materials – reduce cost and environmental impact

if one technology fails could lead to the other contacted tech failing as well

increased functionality of a device may lead to inefficient use

the converged tech may not work as well as on its own e.g. DVD player vs a DVD player in a game console

An example of converging technology is the smartphone.

consider the smartphone as a converging technology in terms of the materials required to create it, its energy consumption, disassembly, recyclability and the portability of the devices it incorporates.

Functionality: telephone. texting, apps, MP3 Player, video and still camera, phone book, etc

Other examples include mobile health devices such as the Fitbit or iWatch or other wearables that have integrated circuits that can monitor body functions.

Wearable Article

Digital Trends on wearables

International-mindedness

The differing stages of economic development of different countries/regions and their past and future contributions to global emissions is an issue.

Theory of knowledge

There is no waste in nature. Should areas of knowledge look at natural processes beyond human endeavour?

CHAPTER THREE

Modelling

3.1 CONCEPTUAL MODELLING

Designers use conceptual modelling to assist their understanding by simulating the subject matter they represent. Designers should consider systems, services and products in relation to what they should do, how they should behave, what they look like and whether they will be understood by the users in the manner intended.

The starting point for solving a problem springs from an idea developed in the mind. A detailed exploration of the idea is vital to take it from the intangible to the tangible, along with the ability to articulate the idea to others

The Role of Conceptual Modelling in Design

Term: A model that exists in the mind used to help us know and understand ideas.

Conceptual models are

a model of concepts or ideas (abstract) that exist in the mind.

used to help us know and understand, design thinking, ideas, casual relationships, principles, data, systems, algorithms or processes.

used to illustrate relationships that is in the designers mind to others.

able to help explain the thinking behind new ideas.

able to help us to communicate with other members of design team, manufacturer or client.

able to help us visualise ideas through graphic, physical and virtual models.

Ever wonder how they know a car park is full?

Car Park Algorithm

Conceptual Modelling Tools and Skills

Term: Graphical Model – A visualization of an idea, often created on paper or through software, in two or three dimensions.

Term: Physical Model – The creation of a smaller or larger tangible version of an object that can be physically interacted with.

Term: Virtual Model – Photorealistic CAD-based interactive models that use surface and solid modelling. They can be considered 'digital mock-ups'.

The the designer visualizes concepts, design thinking and learning with:

Graphical models such as flow charts, drawings and diagrams.

Physical Models with clay, card, 3D printing, foam or wood (easily worked wood like Balsa).

Virtual Models using CAD, simulation and other software.

Flowchart

Graphic Model

Physical Model

Card Modelling Dyson Vacuum Cleaner

Basic Flow Chart Symbols

Virtual Model

Conceptual Models Vary in Relation to the Context

The design context could be systems, service or product design.

Systems DesignService DesignProduct Design

https://www.convergencetraining.com/blog/what-is-a-hydraulic-system-definition-design-and-components

Service Design

Product Design

"is the process of defining the architecture, components, modules, interfaces, and data for a system to satisfy specified requirements". (from Wikipedia)"is a form of conceptual design which involves the activity of planning and organizing people, infrastructure, communication and material components of a service in order to improve its quality and the interaction between service provider and customers". (from Wikipedia)The process of generating ideas and then developing them into a final product to be sold to consumers.

Activity: Which modelling technique would most likely be used in each of the design contexts?

AdvantagesDisadvantages

To help explain features in data sets.

Help with project planning.

Put abstract ideas into a visual understandable form that might not be imaginable otherwise.

Promote communication between designer, design team members, manufacturer or clients.

Gauge peoples' reaction.

Make assumptions that which in reality do not work

may lack details – too simplistic.

scale may distort perceptions or understandings.

materials might reflect the final selection.

Graphic models such as flow charts may be difficult for people to understand.

Theory of Knowledge

In the construction of a model, how can we know which aspects of the world to include and which to ignore?

3.2 GRAPHICAL MODELLING

Graphical models can take many forms, but their prime function is always the same—to simplify the data and present it in such a way that understanding of what is being presented aids further development or discussion. Designers utilize graphical modelling as a tool to explore creative solutions and refine ideas from the technically impossible to the technically possible, widening the constraints of what is feasible.

A graphical model is a visualization of an idea, often created on paper or through software. Graphical models are used to communicate with oneself and others which include design team members, the client an the manufacturer. The architect would use plans (orthographic) for the builders but perspective for the client.

2D Graphical Models

Diagram

Pictorial Flow Chart

Rendered Sketch

Concept Sketches

3D Graphical Models

CAD Model

Perspective Drawing

Isometric

Perspective, Projection and Scale drawings

Term: Projection Drawings – Systems of drawings that are accurately drawn, the two main types are isometric projection (formal drawing technique) and orthographic projection (working drawing technique).

Term: Scale Drawings – Drawings that are bigger or smaller than the real product, but exactly in proportion with product.

Term: Working Drawings – Drawings that are used to guide the production of a product, most commonly orthographical projection, section drawings, part drawings, assembly drawings and plan drawings.

Orthogonal/Orthographic Drawings/Projections

Orthographic Projection

A series of flat (2D) views of an object showing it exactly as it is in shape and size i.e. constructional details.

An orthographic drawing shows all details and dimensions and is usually used as a production/working drawing.

It is a convergent thinking style of drawing.

Orthographic drawings are produced at the final solution stage and are used as working drawings in the realization stage.

3rd Angle Projection

International conventions need to be used, such as, 3rd Angle projection, ISO, scale, units, etc which will be explained in criterion C.

Isometric Drawing/Projection.

An isometric drawing depicts the proposed solution in 3D showing shape and form.

They are drawn on a 30/90/30 degree axis.

More on isometric drawings (projections).

Isometric Axes – image from technologystudent

Isometric Drawing with dimensions

Exploded Isometric Drawing.

An isometric drawing of an object with more than one component that depicts how the parts of assemblies fit together.

The drawing is exploded to show component parts of a product and/or the sequence of assembly.

Isometric drawings are produced at the final solution stage and are used as working drawings in the realization stage

Exploded Isometric of a Pen

Clock Mechanism

Perspective drawing

Term: A set of formal drawing techniques that depicts an object as getting smaller and closer together the further away they are. The techniques are one-point perspective, two-point perspective, and three-point perspective.

One PointTwo PointThree Point

Image from ArtFactory.com

Image from ArtFactory.com

Image from ArtFactory.com

A 3D drawing that realistically represents an object by utilizing foreshortening and vanishing points (usually imaginary ones).

Comparison of perspective drawings with isometric drawings ...

Perspective drawings take into account spatial arrangements, for example, foreshortening, while isometric drawings are constructed to a set angle.

Can be used in the planning stages to communicate what it might look like.

Good for clients who may not understand orthographic or isometric drawings.

Assembly and Parts Drawing

Term: Assembly Drawing – A diagram that shows how components fit together to make a whole.drawings Typically presented in an exploded view.

Assembly drawings show how different parts [components] go together, identify those parts by number, and have a parts list, often referred to as a bill of materials.

Term: Parts (Component) Drawing – Orthographic drawings of the components of an assembly containing details just about that component.

Is a part/component of a a product that is assembled with other components and/or sub assemblies.

Assembly Drawing

Part/Component Drawing

Sketching versus Formal Drawing Techniques

Term: Sketches – Rough drawings of ideas used to convey or refine the idea.

Term: Formal drawing techniques – A type of drawing technique that has fixed rules, the most widely used being isometric projection and perspective drawing.

Activity: What things have caught your attention in this video?

Activity: What things have caught your attention in this video compared to the freehand sketching one?

Sketching or freehand drawings

Are spontaneous representation of ideas on paper without the use of technical aids.

Designers use a range of freehand drawings in the early stages of developing ideas to explore shape and form (3D) and constructional details (2D).

Divergent thinking is prominent at this stage.

Annotations

Explain the thinking behind the visual image represented by the drawing.

They allow the designer to consider the implications of the ideas for further development.

Annotated drawings are an alternative form of expression of ideas that allows one to indicate links between the ideas.

Formal drawings.

Include: orthogonal, isometric, exploded isometric, sectional, parts and assembly drawings which are done with great precision and usually with mechanical drawing aides (ruler, square, compass) or in CAD programs (Autodesk Fusion).

Designers use these drawings at the realisation/development stage where the product is to be made. They are used to communicate to the manufacturer.

Convergent thinking is prominent at this stage.

Advantages and Disadvantages

Type of ModelAdvantagesDisadvantages

Orthogonal

Detailed

Contains all necessary information.

Can construct from it.

Accurate and precise.

Easy to communicate with manufacturer.

Need specialised skills such as using CAD

Specialised equipment needed.

Time consuming.

Not easily understood by a lay person (e.g. client).

Isometric

Shows all views at once

Easy to communicate with manufacturer and client

Not all details are included.

May not look like the real thing because the dimensions are all true.

Need specialised skills such as using CAD

Specialised equipment needed.

Perspective

Looks like the real thing, it is pictorial

Easy to communicate with client

No details – dimensions, etc

Time consuming

Assembly

Easy to communicate with manufacturer and client.

Show how product should be assembled.

Time consuming
Specialised knowledge and skills required.
Freehand
Quick.
Easy.
No specialised skills required.
No specialised equipment required.
Easy to communicate with manufacturer and client.
Allows spontaneous creative (Divergent) thinking.
May not look like the intended outcome.
Lacks details.
Theory of Knowledge:
Are there aspects of the world that are not amenable to modeling?
To what extent does graphical communication shape and limit our knowledge?

3.3 PHYSICAL MODELLING

Designers use physical models to visualize information about the context that the model represents. It is very common for physical models of large objects to be scaled down and smaller objects scaled up for ease of visualization. The primary goal of physical modelling is to test aspects of a product against user requirements. Thorough testing at the design development stage ensures that an appropriate product is developed.

Physical modelling not only allows designers to explore and test their ideas, but to also present them to others. Engaging clients, focus groups and experts to interact with physical models of products allows designers to gain valuable feedback that enable them to improve the design and product-user interface.

Scale Models
Term: A model that is either a smaller or larger physical copy of an object.
Scale models are:
accurate physical representations of objects or features of objects.
able to allow the design team, client or manufacturer visualise and/or manipulate (examine) the object.
scaled down or up keeping all sizes of the features in relation to each other.
Architecture Model
DNA Model
A scaled down model of a large object such as a building, car etc is used to gain a better understanding in the environment it will be in.
A full-sized building is modelled at greatly reduced scale.
This enables designers to visualise the structure of the building, external and internal lines and form.
A scaled up a small object such as a molecule or micro chip in order to be able to clearly visualise it as it is too small to normally see it.
Aesthetic models
Term: A model developed to look and feel like the final product.
An aesethic/appearance prototype or appearance model is as its name suggests.
It does not function or operate in any way.
Aesthetic/appearance models are only concerned with form, color, style, texture and how the product fits in its visual environment.
They can be used for ergonomic testing, evaluating visual appeal, allow the non-designer to see and feel how the real product will be, or production engineers collect data that will help them assess the feasibility for matching manufacturing systems.
Lotus Clay Aesthetic Model

It is usually made from clay, foam, rubber, plastic or wood. For example, a simple model it could solid pieces of foam that has been shaped and painted to look like the real thing or complex models that are like the real thing in weight, balance, materials and material properties.

Aesthetic models can be are expensive to produce (especially the complex ones) because of the life like surface finish but some are life sized like the car pictured. These models need to be handled carefully as they are not designed as working models, mock ups or prototypes.

Mock-ups

Term: Mockups – A scale or full-size representation of a product used to gain feedback from users.

Mock-ups are used to test ideas and gather feedback from users.

They can be either full-scale or scaled models of products

They can have some form of functionality, which means they could be considered a prototype as well.

A good example of how a design begins and gets to the mock up stage. It shows gathering of information to graphical and finally physical modelling.

Canon mock up – notice the lens mount and view finder

Prototypes

Term: Prototypes – A sample or model built to test a concept or process, or to act as an object to be replicated or learned from. Prototypes can be developed at a range of fidelity and for different contexts.

Prototypes are to test and evaluate ideas.

A prototype can be a real working product made to real specifications that can be used throughout design development.

It has functionality unlike that of a mock-up (minimal) or lack of it in aesthetic models.

It is particularly useful in testing before production begins.

Prototypes help the development team discover and issues related to manufacturing the final product.

It also allows the development team to learn from the user through user feedback and user trials/interaction with the final prototype.

Prototype Fidelity

Term: Fidelity – The degree to which a prototype is exactly like the final product.

Prototypes can be made at varying levels of fidelity targeting a range of user and environment contexts. A combination of fidelity and user/environmental contexts allows for deeper understanding of the ideas that aide design development. Better understanding of design fidelity.

Model FidelityLow FidelityMiddle FidelityHigh Fidelity

Model Description

Conceptual representation analogous to the idea, for example paper prototypes.

Not really tangible.

The user can offer input into the design idea.

Representation of aspects of the idea, such as, a working mock-up with limited functionality.

This allows the user some interaction.

Mock-up of the idea, as close as possible to the final product, for example a full scale working prototype.

They are tangible and testable.

This allows full user interaction.

Context/Fidelity Level

restricted—in a controlled environment

general—any user, any environment

partial—final user or environment

total—final user and environment

Instrumented Models

Term: Instrumented Model – Prototypes that are equipped with the ability to take measurements to provide accurate quantitative feedback for analysis.

Instrumented physical models are equipped with the ability to take measurements to provide accurate quantitative feedback for analysis.

They can be used effectively to investigate many phenomena such as fluid flows in hydraulic systems or within wind tunnels, stress within structures and user interaction with a product.

For example, an instrumented model of a keyboard can record the actions of the user and provide data on how often keys are used and the number of errors a user makes (that is, the number of times the backspace or delete key is used).

These models can be scaled in terms of both geometry and important forces.

Visit this link on Similitude for another example and extra information.

Instrumented Model Limb – Physiotherapist

Use of instrumented models to measure the level of a products performance and to facilitate ongoing formative evaluation and testing such as the above image illustrates. Find the full report here. Refer to the biodynamics image and website. The study would allow for further design development.

Applications of Physical Models

Product design

Architecture and Engineering

Medical research

Automative industry

Advantages and Disadvantages of Using Physical Models

AdvantagesDisadvantages

Explore and test ideas

Easily understandable

Communication with clients

Communication with team members

Ability to manipulate ideas better than with drawings

Is tangible

Can be used in user trails and user research more readily.

Designers can easily make assumptions about how accurately a model represents reality

It may not work like the final product

Might not be made of the same material

Time consuming to make

Level of skill required

Can be costly (prototypes)

Theory of knowledge

Models that only show aspects of reality are widely used in design. How can they lead to new knowledge?

3.4 COMPUTER AIDED DESIGN (CAD)

As technologies improve and the software becomes more powerful, so do the opportunities for designers to create new and exciting products, services and systems. Greater freedom in customization and personalization of products has a significant impact on the end user. The ability to virtually prototype, visualize and share designs enhances the whole design cycle from data analysis through to final designs.

The use of CAD to simulate the conditions in which a product will be used allows the designer to gain valuable data at low cost. For example, simulating the flow of air across a car exterior negates the need for a car and wind tunnel.

What is CAD?

Term: Computer Aided Design (CAD) – The use of computers to aid the design process.

CAD is using computers to aid the design process, this could include creating and modifying designs (products), graphic design, data processing, analysis (FEA) or simulations.

Types of CAD Software

EHow describes the different software packages.

2D3DRendering

Autodesk AutoCAD

Adobe Illustrator

Autodesk Inventor or Fusion 360

SketchUp

Solidworks

3D Studio Max

Blender

Maya

Fusion, Inventor & Solidworks.

Advantages and Disadvantages of Using Computer-Aided Modelling

Discuss the advantages and disadvantages of using software applications in different design contexts. – Consider product design, architecture and graphic design.

AdvantagesDisadvantages

Changes to ideas can be made quickly and easily.

Communicate with client, manufacture more easily.

Electronically transferred.

Avoid costly mistakes.

Reduce costs as extra prototypes are not needed.

Saves time through efficient work practises.

High accuracy/fidelity.

Software/Hardware costs.

Special training needed.

Steep learning curve.

Dysfunctional Luxuries – Click the link to see more.

The Uncomfortable Design – Clink the link to see more

Surface and Solid Models

Surface Model

Solid Model

Term: Surface Modelling – A realistic picture of the final model, offering some machining data. Surface models contain no data about the interior of the part.

Term: Solid Modelling – Solid models are clear representations of the final part. They provide a complete set of data for the product to be realized.

Comparison of the differences between solid and surface modelling techniques.

Solid modelling techniques contain more information for the designer,

In order to produce a 3D model using CNC (computer numerical control) or RP (rapid prototyping) technologies

Surface modelling only has wall thickness.

Bottom-Up and Top-Down Modeling

Term: "Top down" design is a product development process obtained through 3D, parametric and associative CAD systems. The main feature of this new method is that the design originates as a concept and gradually evolves into a complete product consisting of components and sub-assemblies.

AutoDesk defintion

Term: "Bottom Up" – A designer creates part geometry independent of the assembly or any modelling other component. Although there are often some design criteria established before modelling the part, this information is not shared between models. Once all parts are completed, they are brought together for the first time in the assembly.

This allows for a database of parts that could be used elsewhere.

Is carried out by adding components to existing parts/bodies/components.

Bottom-Up

Top-Down

Data Modelling Including Statistical Modelling

Term: Is a model that determines the structure of data.

Data modelling is based on the data requirements for an application.

This can take the form of a database, an organised collection of data.

Data models structure data through database models. They can be flat file, relational or hierarchical.

A wikipedia reference on Data modelling

Statistical modelling is a mathematical model.

Statistical Modelling

Database

Design of information systems to enable the exchange data

Models of database include ...

Flat File

only contains a single table of data

no structural interrelationship

Relational Database

Two or more tables of data that are linked

It can pull data from different tables and reassembles it.

Virtual Prototyping

Term: Virtual prototyping – Photorealistic CAD-based interactive models that use surface and solid modelling. They can be considered 'digital mock-ups'.

designers can simulate a design visually and/or mathematically

reduce lead times

reduce development costs

reduce or eliminate errors (as humans are not involved)

improve quality

easily scalable – such as in nanotechnology or aeroplanes.

Discuss the cost-effectiveness offered by animation and virtual reality. This helps to reduce full-scale prototyping, which leads to a reduction in tooling costs, labour costs, energy and materials

Digital humans: motion capture, haptic technology, virtual reality (VR), and animation

Digital humans:

are computer simulations of the biomechanics of the human body.

help to predict how a human (real) will react in a variety of situation or environments (places or locations).

Siemens has a great article on using digital humans in product design, manufacturing and so on

Discuss how digital humans can enhance human factors research.

Digital humans can be used to represent joint resistance, discomfort, reach envelopes and visual fields.

They can be used, for example, to measure the impact of clothing on human performance.

Haptic technology (also know as force feedback technology):

is an emerging technology that interfaces the user via the sense of touch.

How it works is by mechanical actuators apply forces to the user which gives them feedback.

By simulating the physics of the user's virtual world, it is possible to compute these forces into real time.

Haptic technology allows the user to become part of a computer simulation and to interact with it, enabling the designer to observe the user's performance and to design a better outcome.

It can be used in different environments particularly ones that are dangerous to humans, remote locations or in difficult locations to train in.

Haptic technology is employed in many gaming (home entertainment) consoles providing feedback such as the Wii Nintendo.

Mashable article on remote surgery

BBC article on remote surgery

Virtual Reality – The ability to simulate a real situation on the screen and interact with it in a near-natural way.

Animation …The ability to link graphic screens together in such a way as to simulate motion or a process.

Motion capture … The recording of human and animal movement by any means, for example, by video, magnetic or electro-mechanical devices.

Explain how motion capture is used to digitally represent motion.

A person wears a set of acoustic, inertial, LED, magnetic or reflective markers at each joint.

Sensors track the position of the markers as the person moves

this produces a digital representation of motion.

Identify the advantages of motion capture for digitally representing motion.

Motion capture can reduce the cost of animation, which otherwise requires the animator to draw either each frame or key frames that are then interpolated.

Motion capture saves time and creates more natural movements than manual animation, but is limited to motions that are anatomically possible. Some applications, for example, animated super-hero martial arts, might require additional impossible movements.

Explain how motion capture contributes to the development of a digital human.

A motion capture session records the movements of the actor, not his or her visual appearance.

The captured movements are mapped to a 3D model (human, giant robot) created by a computer artist, to move the model in the same way.

How haptic technology, motion capture, VR and animation can be used to simulate design scenarios and contexts

Compare animation and virtual reality. – Refer to different design contexts. Consider costs, client needs and development time.

Describe haptic technology.-

Also known as force feedback technology. Haptic technology works by using mechanical actuators to apply forces to the user.

By simulating the physics of the user's virtual world, it is possible to compute these forces into real time.

Explain how haptic technology and motion capture have enhanced design capability.-

Haptic technology allows the user to become part of a computer simulation and to interact with it, enabling the designer to observe the user's performance, so as to design a better outcome.

Haptic technology can also be used in situations where it may prove difficult to train in the real environment.

Haptic technology is also used in feedback devices used in home entertainment consoles.

Motion capturing a number of users' movements will allow designers to design better ergonomic products.

Motion capture allows the designer to understand the users' physiological requirements.

Finite element analysis (FEA)

FEA …The calculation and simulation of unknown factors in products using CAD systems. For example, simulating the stresses within a welded car part.

FEA of a bike frame

FEA of a chair – click the image for more

Compare FEA with testing physical models

Compare finite element analysis with real-life testing.

when testing vehicles consider

costs

type of environment,

weather

the user.

Use of FEA systems when designing and developing products

Explain how FEA can be used to show the forces acting upon an object while in use.

the maximum load of a vehicle and the stresses acting upon the vehicle

from the differences in terrain.

allow to redesign areas of weakness discovered through FEA

International Mindedness:

Improved communication technologies allow designs to be developed collaboratively by different global teams on a 24/7 basis.

Theory of knowledge:

How is new knowledge acquired through the use of digital models?

Does technology allow us to gain knowledge that our human senses are unable to gain?

3.5 RAPID PROTOTYPING

The growth in computing power has had a major impact on modelling with computer-aided manufacture. Rapid software and hardware developments allow new opportunities and exciting new technologies to create dynamic modelling of ever-greater complexity. Models can be simulated by designers using software, tested and trialled virtually before sending to a variety of peripheral machines for prototype manufacture in an ever-increasing range of materials. The ease of sending this digital data across continents for manufacture of prototypes has major implications for data and design protection.

The increasing effectiveness of rapid prototyping techniques in terms of both cost and speed enables designers to create complex physical models for testing.

Rapid Prototyping (RP) and RP Machines

entails a machine that produces a complete product including internal details, at a fairly quick rate.

reduce product development time as prototypes are quickly made and can be tested

one-off products are made for different or specialised situations

is an additive manufacturing technique as opossum to subtractive manufacturing (mills, lathes, etc).

less waste (good for environment and save money)

Explain a situation in which it would be advantageous to use subtractive or additive manufacturing when making a product.

Additive vs Subtractive Manufacturing: Which is Right for You? article gives examples and reasons.

Another article further explaining when to choose

Reasons to consider are, price, speed, precision and complexity, materials, quantity, function (performance) of part.

RP Process

Using CAD software produce a full scale model

Export or convert model in STL (Standard Triangle Language and Standard Tessellation Language).

send to RP machine

manufacture the item

clean up the item

Stereolithography

Stereolithography (SLA) is a 3D printing process.

that uses a vat of photosensitive resin and a vertically moving platform.

It uses a laser beam, directed onto the surface of the photosensitive resin, to print the pattern of the current model layer by hardening the photosensitive resin.

The platform then moves down by a layer thickness so the next layer can be printed.

Also known as optical fabrication, photo-solidification, solid free-form fabrication and solid imaging.

Used for producing models & prototypes, casting patterns, production parts and products.

Laminated object manufacturing (LOM)

LOM machines take the sliced CAD data from the 3D model and cut out each layer from a roll of material, using a laser or plotter cutter. These sliced layers are glued together to form the model, which is either built on a movable platform below the machine or on pins when using card. (IB TSM 2015)

A rapid prototyping systems that creates a 3D product by manufacture (LOM) converting it into slices, cutting the slices out and joining the slices together

Fused deposition modelling (FDM)

An FDM machine is

A heated extrusion nozzle (extruder) that moves through the x & y axis

A plastic (such as ABS, PLA), metal or composite (such as30% metal, bamboo, etc fill PLA) filament is fed through he extruder

basically a CNC robot that holds a small extrusion head. The extrusion head moves back and forth along a platform, building up a 3D model by feeding heated plastic wire through the extrusion head.

Either the platform or extruder move through the Z axis place a layer if build material

Controlled by CAM software.

Selective laser sintering (SLS)

SLS is a 3D printing process based on sintering.

A high powered CO2 laser is used to sinter a thin layer of heat-fusible powder that gradually builds up the 3D model.

Powders include, plastic, metal, ceramics and glass

Types of 3D printing (RP) techniques

Describe different design contexts where SLS, LOM and FDM would be applicable.- Consider quality, cost and accuracy of outcome.

Advantages and disadvantages of rapid prototyping techniques

AdvantageDisadvantage

Product design

More intricate

many prototypes can be quickly and accurately produced

prototypes can be used in user trials

Time/Speed

reduced design development time

changes to ideas can be quickly done

Slow process -have to build internal structure, supports and raft.

Slower that other CAM techniques – e.g. CNC routing, laser cutting, etc

Cost

reduce design development costs

reduce costly mistakes

initial capital cost can be high

Accuracy

increased complexity of designs

parts produced with finer tolerances

can produce intricate designs better other CAM processes

Waste

No or minimal waste – it is additive manufacturing. Other CAM techniques a subtractive.

Volume production

not suitable as it is slow. Other cam techniques would be better suited for volume.

this can be due to the need to build the internal structure.

Materials

A wide range of materials can be used.

Advantage over other CAM processes which are limited in their material use.

Communication

improved with the client, designer and the manufacturer

changes to ideas can be easily communicated

Size

limited to size of the bed or work area – may result in numerous parts (sub assemblies)

not suited for large scale applications

Sample Questions:

Explain the benefits of being able to rapid prototype a product instead of using other CAM techniques. – Consider product design, speed, time, costs, accuracy and waste.

Compare SLS, LOM and FDM rapid prototype processes. – Consider speed, time, costs, accuracy and surface finish.

Discuss the limitations of rapid prototyping for volume-produced products. – Consider the internal structure of a product, and number of components.

Discuss how rapid prototyping (RP) benefits trials, testing and final part manufacture. – Consider reduced development time and costs, and user trials.

International-mindedness:

The high cost of some new processes does not allow for their rapid dissemination globally.

Theory of knowledge:

Which ways of knowing do we use to interpret indirect evidence gathered through the use of technology?

Something Extra

Some 3D printing Links

3D printed vertebra

SLS (3D printed) rocket parts for NASA

3D printed skull for a 3yr old Chinese girl and a 22 yr old Netherlands women.

CHAPTER FOUR

Raw Materials to Final Production

4.1 PROPERTIES OF MATERIALS

The rapid pace of scientific discovery and new technologies has had a major impact on material science, giving designers many more materials from which to choose for their products. These new materials have given scope for "smart" new products or enhanced classic designs. Choosing the right material is a complex and difficult task with physical, aesthetic, mechanical and appropriate properties to consider. Environmental, moral and ethical issues surrounding choice of materials for use in any product, service or system also need to be considered.

Materials are often developed by materials engineers to have specific properties. The development of new materials allows designers to create new products, which solve old problems in new ways. For example, the explosion of plastic materials following the second world war enabled products to be made without using valuable metals.

Physical Properties

Mass

Term: Relates to the amount of matter that is contained with a specific material. It is often confused with weight understandably as we use Kg to measure it. Mass is a constant whereas weight may vary depending upon where it is being measured.

Weight

Term: Relies on mass and gravitational forces to provide measurable value. Weight is technically measure as a force, which is the Newton, i.e. a mass of 1 Kg is equivalent to 9.8 Newton [on earth].

Read the section on Mass from Wikipedia

Volume

Term: The quantity of three-dimensional space enclosed by a boundary, for example, the space that a substance solid, liquid, gas, or shape occupies or contains.

Density

Term: The mass per unit volume of a material. Its importance is in portability in terms of a product's weight and size. Design contexts include, pre-packaged food (instant noodles) is sold by weight and volume, packaging foams.

Design contexts include:

any other context where weight and volume are important.

pre-packaged food (instant noodles) is sold by weight and volume is important.

packaging foams/material volume is important.

Electrical Resistivity

Term: The measure of a material's ability to conduct electricity. A material with low resistivity will conduct electricity well.

It is important when selecting materials as conductors or insulators

Design contexts include: electrical plugs.

Electrical Insulator

Term: Reduces transmission of electric charge.

Thermal Conductivity

Term: A measure of how fast heat is conducted through a slab of material with a given temperature difference across the slab.

It is important for objects that will be heated or must conduct or be insulated against heat gain or loss.

Design contexts include: pots & pans.

Thermal Expansion (expansivity)

Thermal Expansion

Term: A measure of the degree of increase in dimensions when an object is heated. This can be measured by an increase in length, area or volume. The expansivity can be measured as the fractional increase in dimension per kelvin increase in temperature.

It is important when two dissimilar materials are joined. These may then experience large temperature changes while staying joined.

Different materials (even within the same material group eg metals) expand at different rates.

Design contexts include: oven doors, glass pot lids with metal rims.

Hardness

Term: The resistance a material offers to penetration or scratching.

Design contexts include: ceramic floor tiles that extremely hard and resistant to scratching.

Mechanical Properties

Tensile Strength

Term: The ability of a material to withstand pulling (apart) forces.

It is important in selecting materials to resist stretching.

Design contexts include: ropes (climbing or towing), cables (in elevators) and fishing lines.

https://www.youtube.com/watch?v=CeOklEyUw0I

Compressive Strength

Compression

Term: The ability of a material to withstand being pushed or squashed.

Design contexts include: ceramic floor tiles, concrete and bricks for buildings or anything that requires to bear weight.

Stiffness

Term: The resistance of an elastic body to deflection by an applied force.

Stiffness and wing flex – Check out the blog

It is important for maintaining shape is an important performance.

Design contexts include; aircraft wing, diving boards or panels on cars.

Toughness

Term: The ability of a material to resist the propagation of cracks.

Toughness

It is important where abrasion and cutting may take place.

Design contexts include:

any design context where impact is likely.

automobile bumpers

Brittle (Brittleness)

Term: Breaks into numerous sharp shards.

Typically has low toughness.

Design contexts include: glasses

Ductility

Term: The ability of a material to be drawn or extruded into a wire or other extended shape.

It is important when metals are extruded (extrusion).

Typically has high toughness.

Design contexts include production of extended extrusions.

(not to be confused with malleability: the ability to be shaped plastically – see in below section).

Stress/Strain

Stress

Term: The load on a structural member divided by its cross-sectional area is called the "stress in the member".

Strain

Term: The response of a material due to stress, defined as the change in length divided by the original length.

Young's Modulus

Term: A measure of the stiffness of an elastic material and defined by stress/strain.

Stress/Strain Graph (Curve)

The elastic region is generally a straight line.

At the limit of proportionality it changes to a curved line which becomes the plastic region.

Every material will perform differently under the application of stress and therefore each material's graph will be different.

We can identify and collect considerable amounts of information from a Stress-Strain graph.

It is important when selecting materials.

Important to intensify features of the stress/strain curve.

Important to identify Stress/strain curve of various material groups.

Features of a Stress/Strain CurveStress/Strain Graphs for Ductility/Stiffness

Elasticity (Elastic region)

Term: The extent to which a material will return to its original shape after being deformed.

A material behaves elastically, when the stress on the material is released before it breaks, the extension (strain) relaxes and the material returns to its original length or shape.

If you squash a drinking

Elastic video clip

Plasticity (Plastic region)

Term: The ability of a material to be changed in shape permanently.

When bent/deformed beyond yield point and the stress is removed, it cannot change back to original shape.

It maintains the new shape or stretches/tears/breaks.

Plastic Video Clip

Material Selection Charts

Term: A chart used to identify appropriate materials based on the desired properties.

You can drill down to specific materials in these charts.

Material Selection Chart

More selection charts from Cambridge University

NB: Using stress/strain graphs and material selection charts to identify appropriate materials. Students are expected to be able to interpret stress/strain graphs and material selection charts to identify appropriate materials depending on the context.

Aesthetic Characteristics

Term: Aspects of a product that relate to taste, texture, smell and appearance.

Term: Aesthetic Appeal – Favourable in terms of appearance.

What determines aesthetic appeal is when a product is attractive to look at or pleasing to experience. It is through our senses.

Some aesthetic characteristics are only relevant to food, while others can be applied to more than one material group.

Although these properties activate people's senses, responses to them vary from one individual to another, and they are difficult to quantify scientifically, unlike the other properties.

Alessi

Smell: the ability to perceive odours such as sweet, acrid or fragrant

Taste: sour, sweet, spicy.

Sound: related to pitches but also the sound of a crisp apple or a chip/crisp bag that makes a crinkling sound.

Texture: it is how something feels or looks, it can be rough or smooth

Appearance: the design of appearance in a product must be aesthetically pleasing to attract a customer. unless it is for a certain market.

Colour: can be warm (e.g. browns) or cool (eg blues) can have psychological affects (e.g. greens are calming)

Shape: geometric or organic.

Properties of Smart Materials

Piezoelectricity

Piezoelectric materials give off a small electrical discharge when deformed.

When an electric current is passed through it, it increases in size (up to a 4% change in volume).

These materials are widely used as sensors in different environments.

Piezoelectric materials can be used to measure the force of an impact, for example, in the airbag sensor on a car. The material senses the force of an impact on the car and sends an electric charge to activate the airbag.

Airbag system

Shape memory

Shape memory alloys (SMA) are metals that exhibit pseudo-elasticity and shape memory effect due to rearrangement of the molecules in the material.

Pseudo-elasticity occurs without a change in temperature. The load on the SMA causes molecular rearrangement, which reverses when the load is decreased and the material springs back to its original shape. The shape memory effect allows severe deformation of a material, which can then be returned to its original shape by heating it.

Design contexts include frames of glasses, medical tools and antennas for mobile phones.

Robotic limbs (hands, arms and legs) use shape memory properties.. It is difficult to replicate even simple movements of the human body, for example, the gripping force required to handle different objects (eggs, pens, tools).

SMAs are strong and compact and can be used to create smooth, lifelike movements. Computer control of timing and size of an electric current running through the SMA can control the movement of an artificial joint.

Other design challenges for artificial joints include development of computer software to control artificial muscle systems, being able to create large enough movements and replicating the speed and accuracy of human reflexes.

Photochromicity

Photochromicity refers to a material that can described as having a reversible change of colour when exposed to light.

A chemical either on the surface of the lens or embedded within the glass reacts to ultraviolet light, which causes it to change form and therefore its light absorption spectra.

Design contexts include: One of the most popular applications is for colour-changing sunglass lenses, which can darken as the sun brightens.

Magneto-rheostatic & Electro-rheostatic

Electro-rheostatic (ER) and magneto-rheostatic (MR) materials are fluids that can undergo dramatic changes in their viscosity.

They can change from a thick fluid to a solid in a fraction of a second when exposed to a magnetic (for MR materials) or electric (for ER materials) field, and the effect is reversed when the field is removed.

Design contexts include :

MR fluids for use in car shock absorbers, damping washing machine vibration, prosthetic limbs, exercise equipment and surface polishing of machine parts.

ER fluids have mainly been developed for use in clutches and valves, as well as engine mounts designed to reduce noise and vibration in vehicles.

Thermoelectricity

Thermoelectricity is, at its simplest, electricity produced directly from heat. It involves the joining of two dissimilar conductors that, when heated, produce a direct current.

Design contexts include: Thermoelectric circuits have been used in remote areas and space probes to power radio transmitters and receivers.

International mindedness

Smart materials are likely to be developed in specific regions/countries and their benefits can be limited globally in the short term.

Something Extra ...

Watch the other smart material videos from the above PBS series.

Overview of Properties

4.2 A METALS AND METALLIC ALLOYS

Typically hard and shiny with good electrical and thermal conductivity, metals are a very useful resource or the manufacturing industry. Most pure metals are either too soft, brittle or chemically reactive for practical use and so understanding how to manipulate these materials is vital to the success of any application.

Extracting metal from ore

Extraction takes place locally with added value often occurring in another country. (Int Mind). Australia has an abundance of Iron ore which is mined and then shipped to China and Japan where is it made into steel. Iron ore is 81 USD per tonne and Steel 672 per tonne in October 2014.

Grain size (Metals)

Metals are crystalline structures comprised of individual grains.

Grain Size

Grain Size

Zinc grains on galvanised iron

The grain size can vary and be determined by the heat treatment.

Reheating a solid metal or alloy allows the grains to change their structure.

Slow cooling forms larger grains

Rapid cooling (quench) forms smaller grains.

Directional properties can be formed by selectively cooling one area of the solid.

Grain size in metals can affect the properties:

tensile strength – coarse grains the stronger a metal

toughness – large or coarse grains the tougher the metal

ductility – coarse grains the more ductile a metal

brittleness – the smaller the grains the more brittle the metal

flexibility/malleability – coarse grains the more malleable a metal

can affect density

Modifying physical properties

Alloying

Alloys are a mixture that contains at least one metal.

It can be two or more metals such as Bronze: Cu + Sn

It can be a metal and non metal such as Carbon Steels: FE + C

Alloying and foreign atoms

Alloys compared to pure metals

Alloying increases strength and hardness

Alloying reduces malleability and ductility, of alloys compared to pure metals.

This is due to the presence of "foreign" atoms which interfere with the movements of atoms in the crystals during plastic deformation

Work hardening (Cold working or Strain Hardening)

Is the process of toughening the a metal through plastic deformation.

Metals work-harden after being plastically deformed, much like when you twist a soft drink can back and forward and then it get gets stiff and then eventually fails (breaks).

Tempering

Tempering is a heat treatment process

Usually carried out after hardening of a metal to:

increase its toughness and ductility

decrease hardness and brittleness

Remember a hard material will have low toughness and vice versa.

Design criteria for super alloys

Superalloys: is an alloy that exhibits excellent mechanical strength, resistance to thermal creep deformation, good surface stability and resistance to corrosion.

Superalloys can be used at high temperatures, very close to their melting point. The strength of most metals decreases as the temperature increases.

Super alloys are used in Aerospace (e.g. rockets), Aviation (e.g. turbines), Chemical processing industry, nuclear reactors and much more.

Two criteria for super alloys are creep and oxidation resistance.

Creep

Creep is the tendency of a metal (or material) to slowly move or deform permanently due to the long term exposure of stress that are below the yield strength or ultimate strength of the metal. Creep is more severe when metals are subjected to near the melting point heat for long periods of time. (Wikipeadia 2007)

Oxidation resistance

Oxidation is the interaction between oxygen and different substances when they make contact, such as rust Fe_2O_3

Oxidation resistance is the ability of a material to resist the direct and indirect attack of oxygen (oxidation) and degradation.

Recovery and disposal

Of metals and metallic alloys

Metals and metallic alloys are so widely used.

They are easily recyclable

They can be indefinitely recycled

It can reduce the emissions and the affect on the environment

Reduce energy required to produce new metals

fro example up to 95% energy savings in using recycled Aluminium.

Design Contexts

Ferrous Alloys contain iron (makes them magnetic). Non-ferrous contains no iron.

Where different metals and metallic alloys are used

Ferrous Alloys

Mild Steel – Carbon content of 0.1 to 0.3% and Iron content of 99.7 – 99.9%. Used for engineering purposes and in general, none specialised metal products.

Stainless Steel – Made up of Iron, nickel and chromium. Resists staining and corrosion and is therefore used for the likes of cutlery and surgical instrumentation.

Cast Iron – carbon 2 – 6% and Iron at 94 to 98%. Very strong but brittle. Used to manufacture items such as engine blocks and manhole covers.

Non-ferrous Alloys

Aluminium – An alloy of aluminium, copper and manganese. Very lightweight and easily worked. Used in aircraft manufacture, window frames and some kitchen ware. Pure Aluminium can be used in drink cans.

Copper – Copper is a natural occurring substance. The fact that it conducts heat and electricity means that it is used for wiring, tubing and pipe work.

Brass – A combination of copper and zinc, usually in the proportions of 65% to 35% respectively. Is used for ornamental purposes and within electrical fittings.

Silver – Mainly a natural substance, but mixing with copper creates sterling silver. Used for decorative impact in jewellery and ornaments, and also to solder different metals together.

Lead – Lead is a naturally occurring substance. It is heavy and very soft and is often used in roofing, in batteries and to make pipes. (from CastleMetalsEurope)

International Mindedness

Extraction takes place locally with added value often occurring in another country.

Theory of Knowledge

How does classification and categorization help and hinder the pursuit of knowledge?

4.2B TIMBER

Timber is a major building material that is renewable and uses the Sun's energy to renew itself in a continuous cycle. While timber manufacture uses less energy and results in less air and water pollution than steel or concrete, consideration needs to be given to deforestation and the potential negative environmental impact the use of timber can have on communities and wildlife.

Structure of Natural Timber

Softwood and Hardwood Cell structure NB: you need to just be aware of the difference.

Natural timber is a natural composite material comprising cellulose fibres in a lignin matrix.

Moisture content of natural timber

When living trees are cut down the timber is of very little use in engineering, product design and so on. This is due to the moisture (or greenness) of the wood. Most of this moisture needs to be removed and a equilibrium moisture content achieved. In order to achieve this timber needs to be seasoned.

Absorbed moisture is the moisture contained in the cell walls of timber.

Free moisture is the moisture contained within the cell cavities and intercellular spaces.

Equilibrium Moisture content (EMC): This is when the moisture content of wood is at equilibrium (same as) the local environment. This can be affected by humidity and temperature changes.

Seasoning

Seasoning is the commercial drying of timber which reduces the moisture content of wood.

Thus making the timber highly useable.

Kiln seasoning is carried out in a thermally insulated chamber, a type of oven, that produce the appropriate temperatures to complete the processes, such as hardening, drying, or chemical changes.

Air-drying: Air- drying are stacks of sawn timber in the open or in large sheds. There is little control over the drying process as the weather elements have affects.

Kiln-drying are stacks of sawn timber in a kiln, to reduce the moisture content in wood, where the heat, air circulation, and humidity is closely controlled.

Kiln Seasoning

Kiln Seasoning

Air Seasoning

Air Seasoning

Timber Defects

While the moisture content of 'wet' timber is being removed defects may occur, some of which are listed below. Controlled seasoning can avoid this. However, once the EMC is achieve is timber goes from high humidity to low humidity (uncontrolled) then the defects will occur.

Warping is the distortion in wood caused by uneven drying, which results in the material bending or twisting.

Bowing is the warping along the length of the face of the wood.

Cupping is the warping across the width of the face of wood, in which the edges are higher or lower than the centre.

Twisting is the warping where the two ends of a material do not lie on the same plane.

Knots are imperfections in timber, caused by the growth of branches in the tree that reduces its strength.

Timber Defects

Natural timber

Is timber that is sawn from the tree and is used as is (ie not made into plywood, etc). This includes hardwood and softwood trees.

Hardwood trees

The wood from a deciduous (broadleaved) tree.

includes eucalyptus, elm, maple, oak, and beech.

Softwood trees

The wood from a coniferous (evergreen) tree.

includes are pine, cedar, and cypress

Eucalyptus Tree

Pine Tree

Characteristics of natural timber

Tensile Strength: The tensile strength of natural timber is greater along the grain than across the grain.

Resistance to damp environments: is very resistant.

Longevity: Hardwoods very good. Softwoods good.

Aesthetic properties: natural colours range (red, purple, cream and brown). The grain can add to its aesthetics.

Grain Direction

Man-made timbers

Also known as Engineered board or composite wood

Man-made timber include:

Plywood (Laminated boards) are layers of veneers (very thin slices of wood) glued together perpendicularly.

Particle board (Chipboard) which is made from different sizes of wood chips, joined with glue and pressed.

MDF (Medium Density Fibre Board) strands of fibre ruled together and pressed into sheets.

Man-made timber often requires finishing such as painting or lamination.

Lamination is the covering the surface with a thin sheet of another material (plastic laminate, wood veneer, etc) typically for protection, preservation or aesthetic reasons.

MDF

Particle Board

Plywood

Characteristics of man-made timber

Tensile strength: depends on the man-made timber

Plywood – high tensile strength in all directions

Particle board and MDF – very low

Resistance to damp environments: depends on the man-made timber.

Exterior plywood – excellent.

Interior plywoods very low

Particle board and MDF – very low

Longevity:

Plywood is high

Particle board and MDF is low to medium

Aesthetic properties:

Plywood if the top layer is of a nice timber like Beech will be good

Particle board and MDF requires finishing or a sheet of lamination (see previous section)

Treating and finishing timbers

Treatment of wood can involve using solutions. The reasons for treating or finishing wood include:

Reducing attack by insects, fungus and marine borers by making the wood poisonous

Creosote: A material that penetrates the timber fibres protecting the integrity of the wood from attack from borer, wood lice and fungal attack.

Protection from the weather

Protection from Dry rot.

Where timber is subjected to decay and attack by fungus.

Improving chemical resistance

Enhancing aesthetic properties

Modifying other properties

Staining Timber

Insect Attack

Sanding/abrading

Recovery and disposal of timbers

Wood recycling is the process of turning waste timber into usable products.

Recycling timber is a practice that was popularized in the early 1990s as issues such as deforestation and climate change prompted both timber suppliers and consumers to turn to a more sustainable timber source.

Reforestation is the process of restoring tree cover to areas where woodlands or forest once existed. If this area never returns to its original state of vegetative cover the destructive process is called deforestation.

Design contexts

Structural design contexts

Buildings – framing for walls or roofs.

Flooring – would typically use hardwoods because of aesthetics and their longevity (durability).

Aesthetic design contexts.

Furniture

Children's toys.

International Mindedness

The demand for high-quality hardwoods results in the depletion of ancient forests in some regions/countries impacting on the environment in multiple ways.

Theory of Knowledge

Designers are moving from exploitation

of resources towards conservation and sustainability. Is the environment at the service of man?

4.2C GLASS

The rapid pace of technological discoveries isvery evident in the manufacture and use of glassin electronic devices. Different properties havebeen presented in glass for aesthetic or safety considerations for many years but the future of glass seems to be interactivity alongside electronic systems. The structure of glass is not well understood, but as more is learned, its use is becoming increasingly prominent in building materials and structural applications.

Bendable Glass

Glass

The Story of glass, includes recycling and applications.

The Corning Museum of Glass

Glass is primarily composed from silca sand (silicon dioxide) together with limestone (calcium carbonate) and Soda Ash (sodium carbonate) and small quantities of a few other chemicals.

It takes a great amount of energy to produce glass from sand, melting point around 1700 Celsius so scrap glass is added. This makes recovery of glass important. Adding scrap glass makes the process more economical.

Characteristics of glass

Transparency, allows light to pass through thus allowing you to see the contents of a jar or through a window.

Colour, colour can de deigned in my adding chemicals

Strength – low tensile strength but high compressive strength

Brittleness, it has a low impact strength and thus will shatter easily (low toughness).

Hardness, high hardness and wont scratch readily.

Un-reactivity – is chemically inert so leaching of acid based contents is not a problem.

Non-Toxic due to its un-reactivity therefore suitable for food storage.

Non-porous, thus will hold liquids or stop moisture seeping from outside.

Insulator.

100% recyclable and is continuously recyclable

Applications of glass

Type Of GlassDescriptionApplications

Soda Glass This commercial glass and is the most commonly used. Has medium to low thermal shock in other words it will shatter going from cold to hot or the other way. Window panes, glassware, drink bottles, etc

Borosilicate (Pyrex) Commonly know as Pyrex. The chemical composition of Soda Glass is altered by the addition of oxides which improve thermal conductivity. Cookware, science equipment such as beakers, oven doors and anywhere where heat/cold are crucial to the design performance.

ToughenedIs heated up to the point of melting then blasted with cold air. This makes the outside is in compression and the slower cool interior is in tension. When it is impacted it shatters into little pieces rather than sharp shards. Side windows of cars, shower glass or design contexts where there is a potential for impact.

Laminated It is layers of glass and plastic sheets between them. When impacted the glass fragments are held in place. This prevents cracks from growing Bullet proof glass, windscreens, bank teller windows,

Glass Fibre Is very long strands of glass. Sometimes these are woven into mats and used as glass fibre reinforced plastic when combined with a resin (polymer).Tent poles, fishing poles, car panels, swimming pools.

The list is by no means exhaustive – this website summaries them well.

Laminated glassToughened

Design contexts

There are different types of glass which are used in a variety of design contexts.

Glass Walls

Window panes in buildings

Bullet Proof Glass – notice the layers

Pyrex measuring cup

Side windows of cars

Ornamental Glassware

Recovery and disposal of glass

Recycled glass is known as cullet which is added to new raw materials to make new glass.

It reduces the energy required thus the costs in producing new glass.

When recycled the glass is separated into the same colours groups (due to chemical compounds) then are crushed

.

Improves environmental concerns such as the extraction of raw materials, energy consumption, and reduced pollution.

It is continuously recyclable

4.2D PLASTICS

Most plastics are produced from petrochemicals. Motivated by the finiteness of oil reserves and threat of global warming, bio-plastics are being developed. These plastics degrade upon exposure to sunlight, water or dampness, bacteria, enzymes, wind erosion and in some cases pest or insect attack, but in most cases this does not lead to full breakdown of the plastic. When selecting materials, designers must consider the moral, ethical and environmental implications of their decisions.

Early plastics used from 1600 BCE through to 1900 CE were rubber based. Prompted by the need for new materials following the first world war, the invention of Bakelite and polyethylene in the first half of the 20th century sparked a massive growth of plastic materials and as we identify the need for new materials with particular properties, the development of new plastics continues.

Development of Plastic

Early plastics were rubber based

After the 1st World War a need for new materials which led to the invention of Bakelite and polyethylene.

WWII saw a need for new materials such as plastics, e.g. nylon to replace silk for parachutes.

Some uses of plastic during the war are now in everyday use.

Read this BBC article on the history of plastics

BBC on plastics

Raw materials for plastics

From Technology Student

Technically plastics are referred to as Polymers

Petro-chemicals are the main ingredient for modern day plastics.

Roughly 8% of oil production is due in plastics

The raw material for plastics (mainly oil) is extracted in a country, exported to other countries where conversion to plastics takes place and these are re-exported at considerable added value. (Int Mind)

Bio-plastics – such as polylactic acid (PLA) resin which is made from corn or potato starch – is also biodegradable.

Interesting note on compostability of PLA

Biodegradable eating utensils

Structure of thermoplastics

Thermoplastics are linear chain molecules with weak secondary bonds between the chains.

The Making of the Modern World has an informative article on Polymers and intermolecular bonds

Tecnoelpalo on Plastics including their uses.

General characteristics include:

ductile

low stiffness – squishy water bottles for example

easily injected into a mould

can be reshaped after heating

easily and cost effectively manufactured

Types of thermoplasticsPropertiesDesign Context

PP (Polypropene)

lowest density of thermoplastics

good toughness

resistant to fats

high resistance to temperature

good fatigue resistance

semi-rigid

translucent

recyclable

Buckets, bowls, crates, toys, food containers, juice bottles, straws, coat hangers, furniture eg plastic chairs),

PE (Polyethene)

low stiffness (semi-rigid, flexible)

high toughness

translucent

commonly HDPE and LDPE

recyclable

Water bottles, food storage containers, plastic tubing, light work surfaces, shampoo bottles, flower pots

PET (Polyethylene terephthalate)

high strength

rigid

thermal resistant

recyclable

Soda and water bottles, clam-shelll food containers, fibers (eg polyester), parts made by injection moulding,

ABS (Acrylonitrile butadiene styrene)

high impact resistance

high toughness

dimensional stability

good stiffness

good workability properties

versatile material

repayable – not all centres will receive it.

telephone handsets, rigid luggage, domestic appliances, handles, some helmets (impact), product prototyping,

HIPS (High Impact PolyStyrene)

easy of fabrication

high impact strength

good aesthetics-various colours

rigid/stiff

low cost

dimensional stability

good workability properties

non-biodegradable

toys, kitchen utensil, shelves, signs, product casings.

PVC (Polyvinyl chloride)

Can be stiff or flexible (when a plastizeer is added)

good aesthetics – colours

low cast

non-biodegradable

potable piping, water bottles, cling film, credit cards, toys, shampoo bottles, imitation leather, window frames, rain gutters, garden furniture, binders and even pens – as a wide use

'Sam Suds' Courtesy of Center for Health, Environment and Justice

Structure of thermosetting plastics

Thermosets are linear chain molecules with strong primary bonds between adjacent polymer chains.

This gives thermosets a rigid 3D structure.

Characteristics include:

high stiffness

higer strength than thermoplastics

cannot be reheated and remoulded – it will usually char

Properties of polyurethane, urea-formaldehyde, melamine resin and epoxy resin

Type of thermosetPropertiesDesign Contexts

Polyurethane

It can be hard like fibreglass or soft and spongy

wide range of hardness

good tensile and compressive strength

toughness – impact resistant

good electrical resistivity

good bonding properties

good resistant to damp environments

wheels, wing parts, sponges, finishes (lacquer etc), toys,

Urea-formaldehyde

high (surface) hardness

high tensile strength

good

electrical resistivity

low resistance to damp environments

deterioration of indoor are quality

manufacture of man-made timber (pressed) products such as MDF particle board, adhesives, insulation, wrinkle and shrink resistant textiles

Melamine resin

high hardness (one of the highest)

high chemical resistance resin

medium fire and heat resistant (will decompose under great heat)

resistant to moisture (damp environments)

kitchen ware (plates, utensils), decorative laminates (counter or table tops), fire retardant clothing,Epoxy resin

high thermal resistance

high chemical resistance

high toughness

adhesives, fibre optics, electrical insulators and transformers, craft and jewelry industry

Recovery and disposal of plastics

Nearly all plastics can be recycled it mostly depends on economic, technical and logistical factors

Thermoplastics can be easily recycled.

come in a range of chemical compounds and therefore need to be sorted for recycling

Thermosets not so easy (and expensive to do so)

need to be ground into a powder which adds time and costs.

Often get sent to landfill

Some plastics are not accepted at the recycling plant due to its chemical compound and the facilities capabilities.

Temperature and recycling thermoplastics

Result of heating plastic on the polymer chains

The Increase in temperature causes the weak secondary bonds to break (The heat is sufficient enough to break the secondary bonds but not the primary, covalent, bonds) see above image.

This allows the long molecular chains to slide over each other, i.e. be reshaped into a new product.

When a plastically deformed and allowed to cool it will remain in the new shape due to new secondary bonds being formed.

The nature of the structure of a thermoplastic allows it to be readily recycled.

4.2E TEXTILES

The continuing evolution of the textiles industry provides a wide spread of applications from high- performance technical textiles to the more traditional clothing market. More recent developments in this industry require designers to combine traditional textile science and new technologies leading to exciting applications in smart textiles, sportswear, aerospace and other potential areas.

There are many ethical considerations attached to the production of natural fibres.

Raw materials for textiles

Man-made vs Natural

Natural fibres

Materials produced by plants or animals that can be spun into a thread, rope or filament.

Common examples include:

Wool

Cotton

Silk

Synthetic fibres

Fibres made from a man-made material that are spun into a thread; the joining of monomers into polymers by the process of polymerisation.

Common examples include:

Acrylic, nylon, polyester, lyrca, rayon, acetate, spandex, and Kevlar

Properties of natural fibres

Absorbency – is very high

Strength – low tensile strength

Elasticity – not very elastic

Effect of temperature – will burn but does not melt.

NB: Japanese firemen of the past once wore cotton or wool suits to protect them from fires.

Properties of synthetic fibres

Absorbency – is very low

Strength – high tensile strength

Elasticity – highly elastic (like stockings, socks etc)

Effect of temperature – will burn and melt.

This website has a good table on the source of fibres and their advantages and disadvantages

Conversion of fibres to yarns

Conversion of yarns into fabrics

Conversion of yarns into fabrics:

Weaving

The act of forming a sheet like material by interlacing long threads passing in one direction with others at a right angle to them.

https://www.youtube.com/watch?v=TyhDkd8Iabs

Knitting

A method for converting a yarn into fabric by creating consecutive rows of interlocking loops of yarn.

Lacemaking

A method for creating a decorative fabric that is woven into symmetrical patterns and figures.

Felting

A method for converting yarn into fabric by matting the fibres together.

Ethical Considerations of the creation of textiles.

There are many ethical considerations attached to the production of natural fibres.

The strongest natural silk known to man is harvested from silk spiders and notoriously difficult to obtain, and labour intensive.

In an effort to produce higher yields, scientists have altered the genome of goats so that they produce the same silk proteins in their milk.

Many textiles are made in developing countries and the work conditions of the labour force is often repetitive, low skilled and in poor conditions. See video below.

Recovery and disposal of textiles

a great amount of textile waste is produced each that could go to good use or be a new source of revenue stream

Wikipedia of recycling textiles

Textile Waste

Design contexts

Wool

Clothing – sweaters/jumpers, suits, socks, etc

Upholstery – couches, chairs etc

Rugs

Blankets

Industrial use – padding, structural insulation, mattresses & futons, oil & hazardous liquids clean up pads, ...
Cotton
Clothing – pants, underwear, T-shirts, etc
Bedding/furnishings – sheets, covers, pillows ...
Industrial use – wall coverings, book binding tapes, tarpaulins, threads for sewing ...
Silk
Clothing – shirts, under garments, pyjamas, robes ...
Medical sutures (stitches)
Upholstery & Bedding
Nylon
Clothing – raincoats, stockings, socks ...
Industrial use – parachutes, tents, tyres, ropes ...
Polyester
Industrial use – seat belts, tents, transportation upholstery, ropes, sails, fish nets,
Clothing – underwear, night wear and high pile fabrics.
Furnishings – curtains, drapes, upholstery, carpets and rugs
Lyrca
Close fitting clothing.
Sportswear – cycling, running, etc
Underwear
Smart textiles
Fibre2Fashion website
Wikipedia reference
Sportswear
Smart Textiles in sport
Aerospace
Textiles in Space article
Textiles at NASA
International Mindedness
The economics and politics of the production and sale of clothing by multinationals can be a major ethical issue for consumers and the workforce.
Theory of Knowledge
Designers use natural and man-made products. Do some areas of knowledge see an intrinsic difference between these?

4.2F COMPOSITES

Composites are an important material in an intensely competitive global market. New materials and technologies are being produced frequently for the design and rapid manufacture of high-quality composite products. Composites are replacing more traditional materials as they can be created with properties specifically designed for the intended application. Carbon fibre has played an important part in weight reduction for vehicles and aircraft. (2.2)

What is a composite?

A mixture composed of two or more materials with one acting as the matrix (glue) the other acts as a reinforcement (fibres/sheet/particles).

Particle Board
Carbon Fibre Matting (sheet)
It takes the form of fibres/sheets/particles (reinforcement) in a matrix (glue).
The fibres/sheets/particles can be made from textiles, glass, plastics, wood and carbon.
The matrix can be made from thermoplastics, thermosetting plastics, ceramics (e.g. concrete), metals.
It is made via the process of weaving, moulding, pultrusion or lamination

Composition and structure of composites

Concrete – water, Portland cement, and aggregates (gravel etc)

Concrete

Engineered wood – also called composite wood, man-made wood, or manufactured board. gluing sheets (veneer), particles or stands of wood together.

Plywood – sheets of venner glued together with the grain perpendicular to each sheet.

Plywood

Particleboard – chips of wood glued together (see above image).

Fibreglass – stands of glass, formed into a matt and then covered in resin (polymer/thermoset plastic).

Glass fibre

Kevlar® – para-aramid synthetic fiber covered in a resin

Kevlar

Carbon- reinforced plastic – carbon fibres formed into a matt (see above image) then covered in resin.

Laminated veneer lumber (LVL) – uses multiple layers of thin wood assembled with adhesives

LVL

Advantages and disadvantages of composite materials

Advantages are outlined at this website.

Advantages and disadvantages PDF

Design contexts of various composite materials.

Concrete – skyscrapers, bridges, sidewalks, highways, houses and dams.

Plywood – a wide range of uses from construction, internal (furniture, flooring, etc) and exterior uses (such as marine ply for boats).

Particle board – used in furniture (such wardrobes, wall units, TV cabinets), shelving, toys, and wall linings

Fibreglass – boats, pools, pipes, bathtubs, motor industry (vehicle bodies)

Kevlar – armour, high performance canoes or sports equipment, ropes, military applications, tyres, sails,

Carbon re-inforced plastic – high performance car racing, sports equipment (golf clubs, etc), aviation (the Boeing Dreamliner)

Laminated veneer lumber (LVL) – structural applications such as in buildings.

International-Mindedness

Many composite materials are expensive to produce and their dissemination globally is limited.

4.3 SCALE OF PRODUCTION

Decisions on scale of production are influenced by the volume or quantities required, types of materials used to make the products and the type of product being manufactured. There are also considerations of staffing, resources and finance.

The growing phenomenon of mass customization brings consumers into the design process, allowing them to make choices that make a product unique, to make it their own. Companies have developed "design stations" in their retail stores where consumers can create virtual 3D models, "try them out" using digital technology and place their order.

Production Systems

Craft production – A small-scale production process centred on manual skills.

Mechanized production – A volume production process involving machines controlled by humans.

Automated Production – A volume production process involving machines controlled by production computers

See Productions systems for more details

Craft Production

Mechanized Weaving

Automated Production

One-off Production

Is an individual product or a prototype for larger-scale production.

Products maybe made often with craft production techniques or a combination of craft and machines.

There is a close relationship between the manufacturer and consumer due to the user needs dominate.

If a prototype is made then it is usually part of the realisation of a product and so the next step after testing and evaluating would be batch or continuos flow production.

Examples of products made include prototypes (e.g. car or clothing production), specialist models, hand crafted items (e.g. jewellery, shaker furniture), specialist engineering, specialist architecture (e.g. individual homes, skyscrapers, hotels like the Hydropolis) and just plain old one offs (e.g. Ocean liners).

With CAD/CAM (eg 3d Printing) one-off production can occur in the home.

Advantages

Highly customisable to consumers needs.

Flexibility for the designer and consumer.

Allow for testing of prototypes before continuous flow production.

Disadvantages

Can be expensive as any tools or machinery needed are included in the final cost.

Time consuming if craft manufacturing techniques are used

May be that the product is not designed for disassembly (DfD) there are no interchangeable parts.

Specialist Guitar

Shaker Furniture

Batch Production

It is a limited production run (a set number of items to be produced).

Batch production is a manufacturing method used to produce or process any product in batches, as opposed to a continuous production process, or an one-off production.

Batch production is popular in bakeries and in the manufacture of sports shoes, pharmaceutical ingredients, inks, paints and adhesives.

Can be mechanised or automated production

Greater consumer choice and product differentiation

Advantages

Cheaper than one-off production (economies of scale).

Customisable products but not as highly as one-off production.

Easily adjust to market demands or seasonal items

Greater consumer choice (e.g. Swatch watches).

For smaller or upstart companies that can't afford continuous flow production.

It can reduce initial capital outlay because a single production line can be used to produce several products.

Disadvantages

Down time between productions runs when retooling.

Products have to be stored raising the costs per item.

Mass Production

The production of large amounts of standardized products on production lines, permitting very high rates of production per worker.

Used when large quantities of products are needed such cars, bic pens etc

Continuous Flow Production

Continuous flow is a production method used to manufacture, produce or process materials without interruption.

Is where thousands of standardised products are continuously made 24 hours a day 7 days a week.

It is carried out to maximise production while reducing the costs of starting and stopping the production process.

It can be mechanised or automated process with only a handful of workers needed.

Advantages

Cheaper than other production methods (economies of scale).

If a part or product needs replacing consumer is assured that it still exists (e.g. bic pens).

Lack of inventory which reduces storage costs.

Disadvantages

Standard products so less choice for the consumer.

Automated production is high in initial costs

Training of staff to run machines and CIM

Mass customization

A CIM system that manufactures products to individual customer needs or wants.

It benefits from economy of scale for a single products or thousands of them.

The relationship between the manufacturer and customer becomes closer because the individual requirements of the consumer dominate.

Customise you Nike shoe on Nikeid.

Customised online and shipped directly from the factory

A website dedicated to mass-customisation

His and Her likes

Advantages

Economies of scale are achieved even for small orders

Highly customisable to consumer needs or likes

Disadvantages

Long layover time from with product is customised to reaching the consumer.

Very high initial capital costs

Special training for employees

Design Stations

Custom Apparel

Customizing Levis and #d Printing at Macys!

A Sports Depot with a custom apparel stationCustomising made easy at department stores

Macys Goes Millennial

Custom Laser Bar at Macys

Selecting an appropriate scale of production

Manufacturers choose a scale of production for various reasons

Product characteristics – complexity, features, design, product family, etc

Staff skills – high tech skills for automation.

Financial Considerations – is it cost effective to produce, profits, etc

Material characteristics – plastics are suited to continuos flow production more than say certain metals or other materials.

Size of market – Mont Blanc pens are geared to a market segment which is small whereas Bic pens target are wider market for cheap disposable pens.

Nature of market – such as the variety of products expected by the consumer such as Swatch watches.

Desired manufacturing processes – injection moulding is suited to continuos flow production because it an be fully automated and use cheap thermoplastics

Desired production scale – such as one-off, batch or continuos.

Identify the production methods for certain products in the video.

NB: the above video refers to 'Job Production' which is the same as One-Off Production.

International Mindedness

Mass customization enables global products to become individual items.

4.4 MANUFACTURING PROCESSESS

Designers sometimes engineer products in such a way that they are easy to manufacture. Design for manufacture (DfM) exists in almost all engineering disciplines, but differs greatly depending on the manufacturing technologies used. This practice not only focuses on the design of a product's components, but also on quality control and assurance.

Advancements in 3D printing have resulted in the ability to have a 3D printer at home. Consumers can download plans for products from the internet and print these products themselves.

Design for manufacture (DfM)

Design for manufacture – Designers design specifically for optimum use of existing manufacturing capability.

Therefore if a company has injection moulders available then the designer designs the product with that manufacturing machine in mind – i.e. considers the material needed (thermoplastic) and its related properties and workability.

Additive Techniques

Are manufacturing techniques that add material in order to create a product or component.

3D printing has rapidly advanced and become affordable which has resulted in the ability to have a 3D printers at home.

Consumers can download plans for products from the internet and print these products themselves.

Simple CAD software is more understandable these days so consumers can design and print custom parts.

Paper-based rapid prototyping

Rapid Prototyping with Paper

It lays sheets of regular office paper and cuts out the shapes.

Description from Medium

Materials used: ummh Paper!

Design contexts include: photo-realistic concept and presentation models, design and ergonomic prototypes, durable living hinges, low-cost castings and moulds for vacuum forming .

Design contexts include: appearance models,

MCOR technologies article

AdvantagesDisadvantages

Low cost

Readably available material

Paper has a wood like structure so can be worked or finished by similar techniques

Large parts can easily and cheaply be made

Can be a low capital cost for machine

Use recycled paper

Lower dimensional accuracy (low fidelity) than LOM or SLS when using more traditional techniques (i.e. not MCOR)

In UCD – may not be quite like the intended outcome.

3D printing for paper prototyping can has a high initial capital cost for the machine

Laminated object manufacture (LOM) (see rapid prototyping topic 3)

A rapid prototyping systems that creates a 3D product by manufacture (LOM) converting it into slices, cutting the slices out and joining/gluing the slices together

Materials used: paper, plastic, or metal

Design contexts include: models, prototypes, vacuum forming moulds, pattern (for casting), or one-off products

AdvantagesDisadvantages

no need for support structures

only the shell is produced

capability for high manufacturing speeds

can produce whole products that are hollow

poor surface finish

Stereolithography (see rapid prototyping topic 3)

Materials used: photopolymer (photo sensitive polymer)

Design contexts include: functional parts, pattern (for casting), pattern for various moulding techniques,

Stereolithography aide surgeons for ear implants case study

AdvantagesDisadvantages

Fast – functional parts can be made in a day

Can be machined

Cost of the material a photosensitive resin

Initial capital cost of machine

Subtractive/Wasting Techniques

Are manufacturing techniques that cut away material in order to create a product or component.

Cutting

Is where a material is reduced into he desired shape through sitting away material.

Saws (power and hand held)

Scissors (power and hand held)

Thicknessser/planer, router, (equipment/power), spokeshave, sureform, plane (hand held), oxy-acetylene and plasma cutter (hand held)

CNC (automated) – laser, plasma (can be hand held as well) or water jet cutting

Materials applicable for: wood, plastics, metals, ceramics/stone and textiles.

Design contexts include: Wall clocks, artwork, puzzles, toys, living hinges, flat pack furniture, This website has some more examples.

Advantages/Disadvantages of CNC cutting

AdvantagesDisadvantages

equipment and CNC have a high accuracy

equipment and CNC produce a high quality finish

produce very fine details

minimal distortion

equipment and CNC initial costs are high

special training/skills are required

Band Saw

Hand Saws

Machining

Is the removal of material by a tool that moves across the material by use a machine or large equipment.

Drill press, mill machine, lathes or shaper

Can be CNC (automated) or mechanised

Materials applicable for: wood, metal, plastics, ceramics,

Design contexts include: components or parts for engines, for assemblies,

Drill Press

Mill Machine

Wood Lathe

AdvantagesDisadvantages

High accuracy can be achieved

equipment and CNC produce a high quality finish

produce very fine details

CNC/CAM allows for 24/7 production

equipment and CNC initial costs are high

special training/skills are required

less workers requires in a CNC/CAM work environment

Turning

The material is held between two centres and the tool moves longitudinally across it removing material.

Wood or metal lathes

Can be CNC (automated) or mechanised

Materials applicable for: Wood, metal and rigid machinable plastics (nylon, delrin)

Design contexts include: baseball bats, candle sticks, pens, cylindrical/Conical parts or components for assemblies for industries such as automative or aerospace.

Advantages/Disadvantages see machining

Milling

The material is held firm in a vice on a movable bed and a rotating cutting tool sweeps along the paths on the surface of the material. The bed moves the material around while the cutting moves only through the z-axis.

Materials applicable for: wood, metal, rigid machinable plastics.

Design contexts include: molds for injection moulding, ventilators, pens, paintball guns, rims for tyres, guitars, parts for wooden clocks, etc

Advantages/Disadvantages see machining

Drilling

Is boring a hole into a piece of material. The Material is held firm and does not move and a rotating drill bit moves through the z-axis removing material.

Materials applicable for: wood, metal, ceramics, plastics.

Design contexts include: wooden pens, a hole in the stop of a candle stick, or anything that requires a hole.

Advantages/Disadvantages see machining,

Abrading

Wearing away material using abrasive material.

Sand or abrasive paper, scapers (hand held tools)

Grinders (bench and hand held)

Disk, belt and spindle sanders (equipment and power tools)

Materials applicable for: wood, metal, ceramics/glass, plastics

Design contexts include: used to make things smooth, round edges usually a process used as part of the overall product of a product.

AdvantagesDisadvantages

provides a good finish

takes sharp edges away – safety

Cheap shaping technique – relatively low capital cost

can be noisy so health hazard

can be dusty so health hazard

Shaping techniques:

Are manufacturing methods for modifying the shape of a material.

Moulding

Heat a material until it is a liquid or pliable state.

Then placing into a mould.

Materials used: usually plastic/polymer but can be glass or metal.

Common types moulding ...

Injection moulding

Producing products or parts by injecting plastic into a mould.

Can considered a clean technology as there is little waste.

See below video on the Paton Chair

Materials used include thermoplastics

Design contexts include: plastic garbage bins or tubs, plastic combs, or anything that is usually plastic and mass produced.

AdvantagesDisadvantages

fast production

material and colour flexibility

low waste

design flexibility

high initial capital costs

part and size design restrictions

Blow moulding

Is the process of inflating a hot, hollow, thermoplastic that is inside a closed mould. A blast of hot air is sent in which expands the plastic so it conforms which the mould cavity.

Can considered a clean technology as there is little waste.

Materials used include thermoplastics and glass

Design contexts include: bottles,

Rotational moulding

Heated hollow mould is rotated during the heating up of the plastic and cooling.

Materials used include thermoplastics

Design contexts include: water tanks, buoys, pontoons, toys

Compression moulding

Where the material is heated so it is pliable. It is placed in an open mould that closes and compresses the material to the shape of the mould cavity.

Can considered a clean technology as there is little waste.

Materials used include thermoset plastics and ceramics, Special thermoplastics

Design contexts include: power sockets,

Thermoforming

Where a plastic sheet is heated until it is in a pliable state. Then placing into a mould to form a shape. Vacuum forming is a common method used.

Materials used: thermoplastic

Design contexts include: disposable cups, egg cartons, trays, blisters, clamshells, . e door and dash panels, refrigerator liners, etc

AdvantagesDisadvantages

high speed production

material optimization

Cost effective

material flexibility

low cot of tooling

shape and size restrictions

matching of the edges are required

Laminating

sheets of thin veneer (about 1 mm thick) are layered with a glue (polymer) in-between.

Materials used: glass, timber, paper and plastic

Design contexts include: chairs, plywood

AdvantagesDisadvantages

range of veneers available

strength to weight ratio

Cost effective

flexible in design

time consuming

moulds will have to be made

bends need special consideration

Casting

Pouring a molten material (metal) into a mould. Often the mould is broken. The shape is called a casting.

Materials used: metals.

Design contexts include: sculpture, parts for cars (engines etc), marine propellors

AdvantagesDisadvantages

complex shapes can me made

cost-effective

flexible in size (really big castings can be made)

finishing is required

labour intensive for sand casting

Knitting (see textiles)

Yarn is used to produce fabric or textiles. Loops are formed and stitched together.

Materials used: synthetic and natural fibres

Design contexts include: fabric, scarves

Weaving (see textiles)

Weaving is an ancient textile art and craft that involves placing two sets of threads or yarn called the warp and weft of the loom and turning them into cloth. In general, weaving involves the interlacing of two sets of threads at right angles to each other: the warp and the weft.

Materials used: synthetic and natural fibres

Design contexts include: fabric, tapestries, scarves

Joining techniques:

Methods that are used to join two similar or dissimilar materials together.

Permanent

Adhering (or Gluing) – the use of adhesives (glues). One part receives a layer of an adhesive substance, and the second part will be placed next to the object with the sides touching. Once the adhesive dries, the products have been formed into one object, with the adhesive between the two holding them together.

Design contexts include:

Adhesives

Welding

Rivets

Fusing (this includes welding and brazing)

Fusing is a manufacturing technique used to join similar materials together by melting them at high temperatures and usually adding a small amount of a similar material.

Design contexts include: used in combination in producing artefacts. Artwork maybe produced by welding decorative polices together. Construction of steel frames.

Fasteners (Permanent)

include nails, rivets,

Design contexts include: used in combination in producing artefacts. Often used for two dissimilar materials.

AdvantagesDisadvantages

cost effective – low cost

permanent

easy to carry out

Cannot be taken apart if something needs replacing

welding or brazing requires skills

welding or brazing requires specialised equipment

welding or brazing has safety issues

Temporary

Fasteners (Temporary)

The use of fasteners stands for using certain connecting devices to join two or more dissimilar materials together. They can be undone to separate the materials if needed.

Types of temporary include – nut & bolts, screws, keys, studs, pins, rings, rivets and nails, velcro and knock-down fittings.

Design contexts include: to join two or more dissimilar materials together. Used in flat pack (think Ikea) furniture

Adhering

Thermoplastic glue such as that used in hot glue guns

Design contexts include: holding materials or electrical components in place temporarily

Knock down fittings

Velcro

Nuts and Bolts

Appropriate manufacturing techniques

When selecting manufacturing techniques it should be based on the following criteria

Material characteristics such as form, melting/ softening point.

Cost

Scale of production

Desired properties

International Mindedness

More expensive modern processes tend to take place in technologically advanced regions/ countries.

4.5 PRODUCTION SYSTEMS

As a business grows in size and produces more units of output, then it will aim to experience falling average costs of production—economies of scale. The business is becoming more efficient in its use of inputs to produce a given level of output. Designers should incorporate internal and external economies of scale when considering different production methods and systems for manufacture.

The design of a production system requires a complete understanding of a product, its function and the quality of finish. Each system can be unique and specific to the product it is creating, often requiring the designers to adapt their design to be manufactured using certain methods.

Craft production

A production process that based on manual skills. It is a small-scale production.

A Shaker Craftsman

Advantages and disadvantages of craft production.

When discussing advantages and disadvantages, students should consider economies of scale, value of the product, labour, market forces and flexibility of manufacture.

AdvantagesDisadvantages

Economies of scale

Craft production it is not possible to produce on a larger scale.

This could mean a loss of profit for the manufacturer

however the higher prices of craft produced products can sometimes make up for this.

Price is higher as labour, tools, etc have to incorporated in the final cost.

Value of the product

Although the manufacturing process doe not require machines for the producer,

It takes a great amount of time and effort

Therefore it becomes much more expensive for the buyer.

Every piece also becomes more valuable so any defects will be more important.

Labour

Much skill is often required for the craftsman

Therefore they are able to charge more for the manufacturing of the product.

It takes a great amount of time and effort

Slower than mechanized production.

Market forces

A lot more care is put into making the product as good/nice as possible,

Therefore the quality tends to be seen as considerably higher than something that was mass-produced

Flexibility of manufacture

The product can also be customised to fit personal needs

There is a good deal of flexibility for the designer, customer and craftsman.

May be that the product is not designed for disassembly,

so if something goes wrong during the making of it, there are no interchangeable parts.

Therefore it becomes much more expensive for the buyer.

Design Contexts include: one-off products such as custom made furniture, pottery, art and crafts,

Mechanized production

A volume production process where machines are controlled by humans.

Originally, very small numbers of products were made by craftsmen in home workshops.

The increasing demand for consumer goods following the industrial revolution, meant that larger numbers of products needed to be manufactured in a more efficient way

When discussing advantages and disadvantages, consider cost, quality of product, social conditions and labour.

Advantages

The creation of economies of scale ... the product is cheaper than craft production

The quality of the product is improved as fewer human errors will occur, the finish of the product will also be improved.

Increased wages due to training and becoming skilled.

Efficiency of production: less time is taken to produce goods

Disadvantages

Redundancy – machinery for labour substitution

Health and safety. Work conditions are usually poor in the factories, lack of safety standards can be an issue in some cases. Repetitive strain injury.

Cost of energy, training and capital machinery. Increased wages due to highly skilled operators needed.

Environmental pollution.

Boredom for the workers

Low job satisfaction for workers

Design Contexts include: bicycles,

Automated production

A volume production process involving machines controlled by computers.

Systems such as CAD, CAM and CNC can contribute to an automated production system by linking to the manufacturing equipment with is likewise controlled by a computer. CAM for example would offer a better control over the equipment then a human operator, which can also reduce labor costs. Also since the machines are following the exact CAD drawings there is a lower chance of flaws to occur with the finished product. Designers can use this method to create prototypes much faster and it allows them also to test if the product is feasible. Furthermore it allows the production process to lower waste amount.

When discussing advantages and disadvantages, consider cost, quality of product, social conditions and labour.

Design Contexts include: toilet paper, plastic drink bottles,

Many products require such precision in their manufacture that, without automation, it would not be possible to produce them at an affordable price

Computer numerical control (CNC)

(CNC) refers to the computer control of machines for the purpose of manufacturing complex parts in metals and other materials. Machines are controlled by a programme commonly called a "G code". Each code is assigned to a particular operation or process. The codes control X, Y and Z movement and feed speeds.

G-Code for a 3D printer

Assembly line production

A volume production process where products and components are moved continuously along a conveyor. As the product goes from one work station to another, components are added until the final product is assembled.

The mass production of a product via a flow line based on the inter-changeability of parts, pre-processing of materials, standardisation and work division.

The use of an assembly line for manufacturing a product is a manufacturing technique where the product in question is moved from one modification stand to another by a mechanically moving conveyor. It is used to gather in a fast way large amounts of uniform products. The origins of the Assembly line can be traced back to 1908, when Henry Ford invented and used for the first time the assembly line for the manufacturing of his Ford Model T.

Read this item

When discussing advantages and disadvantages, consider cost, quality of product, social conditions and labour.

Design Contexts include: automobile manufacture, computer or laptops, most electronic consumer products.

Mass production

is the production of large amounts of standardized products on production lines, permitting very high rates of production per worker.

Advantages and disadvantages ...

Mass customization

See Mass customisation on 4.5 Production Systems.

It is a sophisticated CIM system that manufactures products to individual customer orders. The benefits of economy of scale are gained whether the order is for a single item or thousands.

Production system selection criteria

Production system selection criteria include time, labour, skills and training, health and safety, cost, type of product, maintenance, impact on the environment and quality management

Impact of different production systems on the workforce and environment

Automation – Consider nature and type of employment, health and safety issues, social interaction and job satisfaction. Short essay on the human impact of Automation

Positive

Tedious and time-consuming jobs are now being performed by machines rather than workers. An example would be dish washing.

Improved health and safety due to improved work conditions

Improved job satisfaction due to improved work conditions

Replaces unskilled workers with skilled workers or upscaling of existing workers. Results in better pay

Negative

Less social interaction in the workplace due to fewer employees

The numbers of workers needed has been cut sharply

The loss of worker expertise

The loss of overtime pay

Makes life dependant on new technology

Training in the new areas of electronics, computer engineering and maintenance of systems is now needed. –HSC Online

huge negative affect on the environment due to heavy industrialisation

Mechanisation and Assembly Line

Positive

More labour is performed by machines

More social interaction since workers are under one roof

Upscaling from craft to learn new machines results in better pay

Negative

Health and Safety may decrease due to pollution from industrialisation

Loss of master craftsman

huge negative affect on the environment due to heavy industrialisation

Craft Production

Positive

High job satisfaction, prestige as a master craftsman

Good health and safety due to control over the work environment

Minimal negative affect on the environment

Negative

minimal social interaction usually working on their own

Design for manufacture (DfM):

DfM means designers design specifically for optimum use of existing manufacturing capability. There are four aspects of DfM.

Design for materials

designing in relation to materials during processing

Design for process

designing to enable the product to be manufactured using a specific manufacturing process, for example, injection moulding.

Design for assembly

designing taking account of assembly at various levels, for example, component to component, components into sub-assemblies and sub-assemblies into complete products.

Design for disassembly

designing a product so that when it becomes obsolete it can easily and economically be taken apart, the components reused or repaired, and the materials repurposed or recycled.

Adapting designs for DfM

Designs will need to be adapted in some way in order to utilise the different DfMs.

These include: using standard parts, reducing the number of parts, employ modular design principles, rude the number of sub-assemblies

International-Mindedness

The geographical distribution of different modes of production is an economic and political issue.

Theory of Knowledge

The increased dependency on automation and robots has affected craftsmanship. How has technology affected traditional ways of knowing?

As a business grows in size and produces more units of output, then it will aim to experience falling average costs of production—economies of scale. The business is becoming more efficient in its use of inputs to produce a given level of output. Designers should incorporate internal and external economies of scale when considering different production methods and systems for manufacture.

The design of a production system requires a complete understanding of a product, its function and the quality of finish. Each system can be unique and specific to the product it is creating, often requiring the designers to adapt their design to be manufactured using certain methods.

Craft production

A production process that based on manual skills. It is a small-scale production.

A Shaker Craftsman

Advantages and disadvantages of craft production.

When discussing advantages and disadvantages, consider economies of scale, value of the product, labour, market forces and flexibility of manufacture.

Advantages:

A lot more care is put into making the product as good/nice as possible, therefore the quality tends to be seen as considerably higher than something that was mass-produced. The product can also be customised to fit personal needs, and there is a good deal of flexibility for the designer, customer and craftsman. Much skill is often required for the craftsman; therefore they are able to charge more for the manufacturing of the product.

Disadvantages: Although the manufacturing process doe not require machines for the producer, it takes a great amount of time and effort; therefore it becomes much more expensive for the buyer. Also, with craft production it is not possible to produce on a larger scale. This could mean a loss of profit for the manufacturer, however the higher prices of craft produced products can sometimes make up for this. Another disadvantage may be that the product is not designed for disassembly, so if something goes wrong during the making of it, there are no interchangeable parts. Every piece also becomes more valuable so any defects will be more important.

Design Contexts include: one-off products such as custom made furniture, pottery, art and crafts,

Mechanized production

A volume production process where machines are controlled by humans.

Originally, very small numbers of products were made by craftsmen in home workshops. But, the increasing demand for consumer goods following the industrial revolution, meant that larger numbers of products needed to be manufactured in a more efficient way

When discussing advantages and disadvantages, consider cost, quality of product, social conditions and labour.

Advantages

The creation of economies of scale ... the product is cheaper than craft production

The quality of the product is improved as fewer human errors will occur, the finish of the product will also be improved.

Increased wages due to training and becoming skilled.

Efficiency of production: less time is taken to produce goods

Disadvantages

Redundancy – machinery for labour substitution

Health and safety. Work conditions are usually poor in the factories, lack of safety standards can be an issue in some cases. Repetitive strain injury.

Cost of energy, training and capital machinery. Increased wages due to highly skilled operators needed.

Environmental pollution.

Boredom for the workers

Low job satisfaction for workers

Design Contexts include: bicycles,

Automated production

A volume production process involving machines controlled by computers.

Systems such as CAD, CAM and CNC can contribute to an automated production system by linking to the manufacturing equipment with is likewise controlled by a computer. CAM for example would offer a better control over the equipment then a human operator, which can also reduce labor costs. Also since the machines are following the exact CAD drawings there is a lower chance of flaws to occur with the finished product. Designers can use this method to create prototypes much faster and it allows them also to test if the product is feasible. Furthermore it allows the production process to lower waste amount.

When discussing advantages and disadvantages, consider cost, quality of product, social conditions and labour.

Design Contexts include: toilet paper, plastic drink bottles,

Many products require such precision in their manufacture that, without automation, it would not be possible to produce them at an affordable price

Computer numerical control (CNC)

(CNC) refers to the computer control of machines for the purpose of manufacturing complex parts in metals and other materials. Machines are controlled by a programme commonly called a "G code". Each code is assigned to a particular operation or process. The codes control X, Y and Z movement and feed speeds.

G-Code for a 3D printer

Assembly line production

A volume production process where products and components are moved continuously along a conveyor. As the product goes from one work station to another, components are added until the final product is assembled.

The mass production of a product via a flow line based on the inter-changeability of parts, pre-processing of materials, standardisation and work division.

The use of an assembly line for manufacturing a product is a manufacturing technique where the product in question is moved from one modification stand to another by a mechanically moving conveyor. It is used to gather in a fast way large amounts of uniform products. The origins of the Assembly line can be traced back to 1908, when Henry Ford invented and used for the first time the assembly line for the manufacturing of his Ford Model T.

Read this item

When discussing advantages and disadvantages, consider cost, quality of product, social conditions and labour.

Design Contexts include: automobile manufacture, computer or laptops, most electronic consumer products.

Mass production

is the production of large amounts of standardized products on production lines, permitting very high rates of production per worker.

Advantages and disadvantages ...

Mass customization

See Mass customisation on 4.5 Production Systems.

It is a sophisticated CIM system that manufactures products to individual customer orders. The benefits of economy of scale are gained whether the order is for a single item or thousands.

Production system selection criteria

Production system selection criteria include time, labour, skills and training, health and safety, cost, type of product, maintenance, impact on the environment and quality management

Impact of different production systems on the workforce and environment

Automation – Consider nature and type of employment, health and safety issues, social interaction and job satisfaction. Short essay on the human impact of Automation

Positive

Tedious and time-consuming jobs are now being performed by machines rather than workers. An example would be dish washing.

Improved health and safety due to improved work conditions

Improved job satisfaction due to improved work conditions

Replaces unskilled workers with skilled workers or upscaling of existing workers. Results in better pay

Negative

Less social interaction in the workplace due to fewer employees

The numbers of workers needed has been cut sharply

The loss of worker expertise

The loss of overtime pay

Makes life dependant on new technology

Training in the new areas of electronics, computer engineering and maintenance of systems is now needed. –HSC Online

huge negative affect on the environment due to heavy industrialisation

Mechanisation and Assembly Line

Positive

More labour is performed by machines

More social interaction since workers are under one roof

Upscaling from craft to learn new machines results in better pay

Negative

Health and Safety may decrease due to pollution from industrialisation

Loss of master craftsman

huge negative affect on the environment due to heavy industrialisation

Craft Production

Positive

High job satisfaction, prestige as a master craftsman

Good health and safety due to control over the work environment

Minimal negative affect on the environment

Negative

minimal social interaction usually working on their own

Design for manufacture (DfM):

DfM means designers design specifically for optimum use of existing manufacturing capability. There are four aspects of DfM.

Design for materials

designing in relation to materials during processing

Design for process

designing to enable the product to be manufactured using a specific manufacturing process, for example, injection moulding.

Design for assembly

designing taking account of assembly at various levels, for example, component to component, components into sub-assemblies and sub-assemblies into complete products.

Design for disassembly

designing a product so that when it becomes obsolete it can easily and economically be taken apart, the components reused or repaired, and the materials repurposed or recycled.

Adapting designs for DfM

Designs will need to be adapted in some way in order to utilise the different DfMs.

These include: using standard parts, reducing the number of parts, employ modular design principles, rude the number of sub-assemblies

International-Mindedness

The geographical distribution of different modes of production is an economic and political issue.

Theory of Knowledge

The increased dependency on automation and robots has affected craftsmanship. How has technology affected traditional ways of knowing?

4.6 ROBOTS IN AUTOMATED PRODUCTION

Designers should consider the benefits of increased efficiency and consistency when using robots in production and be able to explore the latest advances in technology to ensure the optimum manufacturing process is used. However, a good designer will also understand their responsibility to consider the moral and ethical issues surrounding increased use of automation, and the historical impact of lost jobs.

The introduction of robots to an assembly lines had a major impact on the labour force, often making skilled workers redundant in favour of a technician who can maintained equip a large number of robots.

Primary characteristics of robots:

Work envelope: The 3D space a robot can operate within, considering clearance and reach

Load capacity: Within this context, the weight a robot can manipulate.

Single-task robots – can only carry out one task at a time

Multi-task robots – can carry out more than one task at a time

Teams of robots – groups of robots carry out similar tasks

Teams

Machine to machine (M2M) – where wireless and wired systems communicate between devices to share information or send instructions. More information here.

Advantages of using robotic systems in production.

Improve health and safety of workforce.

High accuracy of work – reduced errors and waste ($$$). Quality of final product is up.

Perform repetitive and dangerous tasks

Work in confined spaces.

Perform functions 24/7 leading to higher production

Reprogrammability or flexible

Disadvantages of using robotic systems in production

Expertise needed to operate such systems.

Training of workers required in both operation and maintenance.

High initial capital cost

Robot Generations

This robotee summaries it well

First-generation robots are a simple mechanical arm that has the ability to make precise motions at high speed. They need constant supervision by a human operator.

Second-generation robots are equipped with sensors that can provide information about their surroundings. They can synchronize with each other and do not require constant supervision by a human; however, they are controlled by an external control unit.

Third-generation robots are autonomous and can operate largely without supervision from a human. They have their own central control unit. Swarms of smaller autonomous robots also fit in this category.

They are not industrial but it does illustrate the autonomous interactions with their environment.

When addressing robots in automated production, students are expected to understand the contexts that different robots are used in.

International-mindedness:

The use of robots in automated production can depend on the local cost of manual labour.

Theory of knowledge:

Technology in the form of robots currently serves man. Is man's place secure? Will the nature of man change due to technological enhancement? Will he be superseded altogether by technological developments?

CHAPTER FIVE

Innovation & Design

5.1 INVENTION

Invention by lone inventors or in collaborative, creative teams is at the forefront of design. Designers must not only be creative and innovative, but also understand the concepts that will make a new product viable. A designer must use imagination and be firmly grounded in factual and procedural knowledge while remembering the needs and limitations of the end user.

Inventions are often the result of an individual or group's curiosity about whether something can be done or a problem can be solved. On occasion, inventions are the result of an individual's curiosity about something other than the product that they finally develop. These inventions include microwave ovens, ink-jet printers and Post-it® notes.

Term: Invention – is the process of discovering a principle which allows a technical advance in a particular field that results in a novel/new product.

Famous inventions.

Times 2018 best inventions.

Some inventions by women

Women Inventors

Comic Book Inventions that became real!

10 comic book inventions

Read these:

Coca-Cola

Invention-vs-Innovation

Motivators for Invention

Term: Drivers for Invention –These include personal motivation to express creativity/for personal interest, scientific or technical curiosity, constructive discontent, desire to make money, desire to help others.

Personal motivation to invent.

It could be out of personal interest (a tinkerer) or creative expression.

To assist people and make life better.

Like Mick Ebeling in the video above.

Open University read on inventor Bayliss and his spring driven radio for Africa

Constructive discontent.

Not happy with an existing product, like Dyson in the video above.

Open University read on inventors Dyson (wheelbarrow) and Carlson (Photocopier).

To make money.

Open university read on lone inventor Gillette inventing a disposable razor blade to generate a continuing need.

Inquisitive scientific or technical thinking.

Open University read on the inventor of the Hovercraft. he didn't know whether to class it a boat or plane!

Necessity.

Maybe a new and novel material is developed and so a new tool is needed.

Activity: Find two novel products or inventions (see links posted above or others you may have found). Explain how those inventions include one or more of the drivers listed.

Activity: Watch the above videos. Find another 5 different accidental inventions. Include an image and a 1 line sentence how it was accidental. Post it on the Padlet.

NB: cant watch the youtube videos then follow this link to Accidental Inventions.

The Lone Inventor

Leonardo DaVinci

Term: Lone inventors – An individual working outside or inside an organization who is committed to the invention of a novel product and often becomes isolated because he or she is engrossed with ideas that imply change and are resisted by others.

More in Topic 5.4

The advantages and disadvantages of being a lone inventor

AdvantagesDisadvantages

Full control over the development of their invention.Lack business acumen.

Driven: with a goal of the complete invention of a new and somewhat revolutionary product.May not comprehend or give sufficient care to the marketing and sales of there product.

Have ideas that are completely new and different.Their ideas, because of how different they are are often resisted by other employees and workers.

Are having a harder time to push forward their designs, especially in a market where large investments are required for success.

Are usually isolated, and have no backing towards their design.

Trouble working in teams because of their emotional attraction to their invention.

Intellectual Property (IP)

Term: IP – A legal term for intangible property such as "creations of the mind" such as inventions and designs that are used in a commercial setting. Intellectual property is protected by law.

This include inventions, designs, art, music, literature, etc.

Open University explains IP and Patents

IP

IP

The benefits of intellectual property include:

differentiating a business from competitors

allowing sale or licensing, providing an important revenue stream

offering customers something new and different

marketing/branding

establishing a valuable asset that can be used as security for loans.

Strategies for Protecting IP

IP Symbols

Term: Patents – An agreement from a government office to give someone the right to make or sell a new invention for a certain number of years.

Term: Trademark, ®, or, TM – A trademark is a symbol, word, or words legally registered or established by use as representing a company or product.

Term: Design protection – A simple and cost-effective way to protect an innovative shape, appearance or ornamentation.

Term: Copyright, © – A legal right that grants the creator of an original work exclusive ownership for its use and distribution. Usually for a limited time and within geographical boundaries, copyright allows the creator to receive compensation for their intellectual effort.

Term: Service Mark (SM) – A trademark used to identify a service rather than a product.

Term: Patent Pending – An indication that an application for a patent has been applied for but has not yet been processed. The marking serves to notify those copying the invention that they may be liable for damages (including back-dated royalties), once a patent is issued.

Look at these two topics regarding IP.

Tell the Apple vs Windows story

Apple Inc vs Samsung Inc Court case

First to Market

Term: First to Market – The first product of this type to be rushed onto the market.

When a company or a person has or think they have an innovative idea or product, therefore, will rush to have it onto the market before anyone else.

Open University read on Clive Sinclair's company – pocket calculators, 1980 computer (hooked up to the TV and used a tape).

"First product that created a new market (such as the desktop computer), a product category (such as the portable computer), or a substantial subdivision of a category (such as the laptop or handheld computer)". Business Dictionary definition.

Apple's Patents: they protect every idea that comes across a desk even if it is never intended to be used soon.

Ten First to Market losers!

Saehan and Rio MP3 players

Apple Newton – the first PDA

Advantages of Being First to Market

Leading the competition

before competitors develop rival products

to gain a larger market share

Increased profit

as the product is the first of its type to be released on the market

allowing the company to capture a large market share

Secure brand loyalty

ensuring that consumers are more likely to purchase the iPad

so the product becomes the dominant design

Secure IP

prevent competitors from developing similar products?enabling

the iPad to become the dominant design

Creating a new product category

that creates a new market

that allows Apple to become a market leader

Shelved Technologies

Term: Technology that is shelved for various reasons. Sometimes shelved technologies will be rediscovered or taken off the shelf.

Reasons for shelving technology include:

Social.

Market is not yet ready for change.

Examples, smart glasses, self driving cars or collision avoidance technology

Technology.

Is not resolved sufficiently to introduce the product. In other words the science behind the technology exists but making it into viable product does not.

Examples, smart glasses, flexible phones (flexible glass has been around a while), touch screen smart phones.

Timing.

Products are introduced in a strategic order.

To improve market viability – gain

Cost/Price.

Product is not released until the technology becomes affordable.

Often new technology or products are expensive (first iPhone) therefore there may not be a market (consumers not willing to spend the money – ie value for money)

Dyson shelved smart glasses 10 years before google – The Guardian Article .

Google shelves their smart glasses – The Irish Times article.

International Mindedness

The role of intellectual property and patents in stifling or promoting inventions globally needs to be considered, especially with regard to the inequalities between countries.

Theory of Knowledge

What is the role of imagination in invention? Are there limits to what can be imagined?

Sometimes there are unforeseen consequences of inventions. To what extent might lack of knowledge be an excuse for unethical conduct?

5.2 INNOVATION

Designers will be successful in the marketplace when they solve long-standing problems, improve on existing solutions or find a "product gap". The constant evaluation and redevelopment of products is key, with unbiased analysis of consumers and commercial opportunities.

In order for an invention to become an innovation, the idea of the product needs to be effectively communicated. The communication can take many forms and be between many stakeholders.

Invention and Innovation

Thank you! to The Open University for their content on Invention and Innovation

Term: Innovation – the business of putting an invention in the marketplace and making it a success.

It is making an invention/s useful and successfully entering it into the marketplace.

A microchip is a wonderful invention, on its own it is useless but in a computer system it is awesome!

Apple iPhone used many inventions to make it a successful product in the market place, including iTunes, touch screens, etc (all of which were inventions)

A PBS article on invention versus innovation

A Wired article on invention and innovation

Thomas Edison

Steve Jobs

Nicola Tesla

Activity:

Few Inventions Become Successful Innovations due to the Following Reasons:

Marketability

Low product demand or not readily saleable

Financial support

There is little monetary backing from the organisation or an outsider.

The invention would need more sponsors to financially aid the product.

Marketing

Is the process of getting products from the producer or vendor to the consumer or buyer, which includes advertising, shipping, storing, and selling. Poor marketing strategies or wrong target markets.

Invention would need to be advertised as a product the public would want.

Trends in innovation.

The need for the invention

Examples include alternative energy resources to combat our insatiable need for oil however if oil prices are low or there is a ready supply of oil then the alternative energy invention will not take hold.

Price

Affordable, cost effectiveness or value for money ... therefore it may be too expensive to purchase, or to manufacture and the consumer may not see it worth its cost compared to its use.

Keep in mind, the product's price needs to be equivalent to the income of the specific age group that would buy the majority of the product.

Resistance to change

People and organisations can be resistant and reluctant to change, feeling comfort and security in the familiar thus resist new ideas/products.

Aversion to risk

"Risk aversion is a concept in economics, finance, and psychology related to the behaviour of consumers and investors under uncertainty". (en.wikipedia.org 2007)

Being successful at innovation …

Article from Innovation tools

Categories of Innovation

Open University explains sustaining and disruptive as well as process innovation.

Term: Sustaining innovation – A new or improved product that meets the needs of consumers and sustains manufacturers.

Examples include the wheel and iPhone where 2nd, 3rd … 6th generations/versions of the product have been developed.

Term: Disruptive innovation – A product or type of technology that challenges existing companies to ignore or embrace technical change

Examples include the iPod which changed the way we managed and listened to music. Mobile phones so we were no longer restricted to landlines.

Ipods/Iphones are disruptive

Term: Process innovation – An improvement in the organization and/or method of manufacture that often leads to reduced costs or benefits to consumers.

Example is in the automobile industry such as Ford with the introduction of assembly line production and Toyota with lean manufacturing.

Robots in car manufacture

More on types of innovation

Activity: Students will need to be able to draw from examples of each category of innovation.

Innovation Strategies for Design

Term: Architectural innovation – The technology of the components stays the same, but the configuration of the components is changed to produce a new design.

Putting existing components together in novel ways.

Examples include: electric cars, Sony Walkman.

1970s Sony Walkman.Panasonic Slim Portable Cassette player.The Crosley (retro-styling) tape deck.

Term: Modular innovation – The basic configuration stays the same, but one or more key components are changed.

Making an existing comment better

Examples include a new type of petrol filter, Youtube or Facebook.

The Google's Project Ara – new dream phone

Term: Configurational innovation – A change is made in both technology and organization.

A great read!

Two students project.

Activity: Examples where innovation strategies have been used for products

Innovation Strategies for Markets

Term: Diffusion – is a process where a market will accept a new idea or product. The rate it accepts the new idea or product can be increased by several factors.

A good article from USC in the US

Examples of widely diffused products include the, light bulb, refrigerator (100%), ATM cards, Music CD's (now mp4 format).

Once widely accepted they often become dominant designs.

ATM cards widely diffused.

Term: Suppression – is a process where a new idea or adoption of a product by the market is actively slowed. This may be due to difficulties competing with a dominant design, ambiguity over patent ownership, competing companies actively petitioning against a new product it perceives as threatening, or the natural resistance to an unfamiliar concept.

Diffusion vs Suppression from Open University

Examples include the telephone (land line) when it had to compete with the firmly established (dominate design) of the telegraph(y).

Activity: Examples where innovation strategies have been used for products

International Mindedness

Innovations may have positive consequences in some countries/regions and negative ones in others.

Theory of knowledge

Design is always looking to the future and new development. Do other areas of knowledge have universal, timeless truths or are they continually in flux?

5.3 STRATEGIES FOR INNOVATION

Companies encourage advancements in technology and services, usually by investing in research and development (R&D) activities. Even though the R&D may be carried out by a range of different experts from varied fields of research, the development process is often based on common principles and strategies to identify the direction of development. This methodology structures the R&D of new technologies and services.

Innovation should always occur in context and a deep understanding of the culture as well as the behaviours, needs and wants of the consumer is required.

Act of Insight

Term: Often referred to as the "eureka moment", a sudden image of a potential solution is formed in the mind, usually after a period of thinking about a problem.

Open University on Act of Insight

Such as Newton watching an apple fall and gaining insight in gravitation forces. DaVinci inventing a crane after watching workers trying to lift heavy stone from a boat.

DaVinci Crane

Adaptation

Term: A solution to a problem in one field is adapted for solving a problem in another field.

Open University on Adaption

The principle of how a hovercraft works was adapted the hover lawn mower.

Fly Mo (hover) lawn mower – has adapted the hovercraft design into its product

How a hovercraft works

Technology Transfer

Term: Technological advances that form the basis of new designs may be applied to the development of different types of products/systems, for example, laser technology.

Open University on Transfer

Laser transferred into surgery or audio or data CDs

Laser beam welding

Laser Pointer

Analogy

Term: An idea from one context is used to stimulate ideas for solving a problem in another context.

Open University on Analogy

Sonar modelled on how bats navigate.

Echolocation

Sonar – checking for depth or fish

Chance

Term: An unexpected discovery leads to a new idea.

Open University on Chance

Velcro was developed when a chap walking with his dog found lots of seed pods stuck to his socks and dog. He looked under the microscope and made his discovery of the pods having many little hooks.

Velcro Inspiration and Invention

Close up of velcro

Velcro Advertisement

Technology Push

Term: Scientific research leads to advances in technology that underpin new ideas.

This is where the driving force for a new design emerges from a technological development.

Open University on Technology Push

The Sony walkman is an example. Read the story how behind it by following the link above or from the image. Basically there was no market need for it. A company employee didn't like how heavy and big the current portable players were.

Sony Walkman = Portable music player

© Chappatte – www.globecartoon.com – "Here comes the iPad"

Market Pull

Term: A new idea is needed as a result of demand from the marketplace.

Open University on Mark Pull

The car market which has separate segments for the supermini, family cars, mini-vans, executive cars, sports cars, SUV, and so on.

Activity: Describe one design context for each of the strategies listed above where they have been applied.

Theory of knowledge

Design is continually changing due to its openness to new ideas. Do other areas of knowledge recognize new influences to the same extent?

Something Extra ...

"Technology" Push approaches:

Typified by programs, but not necessarily software programs

Internal development comes up with a patent or a technological device to fulfill the need of a customer

Has high market related risk because application is not known

Has low technology related risk because application is known

Innovation is created, then appropriate applications are sought to fit the innovation

Did the market ask "please give me an iPod with download store" or a camera phone? Most likely not; so this would be a technology push,.

"Market" Pull approaches:

Implemented on platforms

Platforms are open ended and can evolve based on changing needs

Has low market related risk because application is known

Has low technology related risk because solution is not known

When the market asks for better safety features in a car then this would be market pull.

Theory of Knowledge

Design is continually changing due to its openness to new ideas. Do other areas of knowledge recognize new influences to the same extent?

5.4 STAKEHOLDERS IN INVENTION AND INNOVATION

Collaborative generation of knowledge and high efficiency information flow allow for diversity, increased resilience, reliability and stability within an organization. Through participatory research, stakeholders can make full use of the resulting innovation and invention, by transferring findings relevant to the sector in which they are positioned. A designer's increased awareness through shared industry knowledge enhances profitability and policy.

On occasion, the inventor needs to act as both entrepreneur and product champion. The adoption of these additional roles requires a significant amount of learning to take an idea from the mind, realize it and then diffuse it successfully into the marketplace.

The Inventor, The Product Champion, The Entrepreneur

Term: The Lone Inventor –is an individual working outside or inside an organization who is committed to the invention of a novel product and often becomes isolated because he or she is engrossed with ideas that imply change and are resisted by others.

Leonardo DaVinci

Profile of a Lone inventors

Individuals with a goal of the complete invention of a new and somewhat revolutionary product.

Have ideas that are completely new and different.

May not comprehend or give sufficient care to the marketing and sales of there product.

Are usually isolated, and have no backing towards their design.

Are having a harder time to push forward their designs, especially in a market where large investments are required for success.

Their ideas, because of how different they are are often resisted by other employees and workers.

Some argue that DaVinci was a lone inventor

The last lone inventor, the television.

The myth behind a Lone Inventor

Term: The product champion –is an influential individual, usually working within an organization, who develops enthusiasm for a particular idea or invention and "champions" it within the organization.

Steve Jobs

Profile of a Product Champion

Open University on Product Champion

Knows the customers—all of them

Is not too close to a single customer

Has business experience in the domain

Can speak intelligently about the issues

Acts as a good facilitator, works and plays well with others.

Accepts responsibility for the product.

Defends the team's ability to produce the product.

Is willing to make hard decisions.

Treats the team as knowledgeable professionals.

Sets reasonable performance expectations

Communicates with the team, the customer, management, sales, and marketing

Doesn't think she/he is an expert about the market.

Performs ongoing market analysis

Term: The Entrepreneur –is an influential individual who can take an invention to market, often by financing the development, production and diffusion of a product into the marketplace.

Profile of an Entrepreneur

Open university on the entrepreneur

Business acumen

Self-control

Self -confidence

Sense of urgency

Comprehensive Awareness

Realism

Conceptual Ability

Status Requirements

Interpersonal Relationships

Emotional Stability

A brief anecdotal history of Apple that highlights its success because of the different stakeholders.

The 2 Steves

Steve Jobs the Movie is biography that Steve Wozniak says is pretty accurate.

Original 1976 Apple 1 computer

A part of the whole story tells of how the two Steves started Apple. How Steve Wozniak (the inventor) was the tinkerer, inventor and gadget maker. Steve Jobs (product champion) saw a potential in Woz's inventions. Noether of them had any money. Jobs went to a local computer store owner (the entrepreneur) to secure financial backing to build (in the basement of his home) and sell their computers.

Apple Timeline

Comparison Between Lone Inventor and Product champion

The lone inventor may lack the business acumen to push the invention through to innovation.

The product champion is often a forceful personality with much influence in a company.

The product champion may not be the inventor.

He or she is more astute at being able to push the idea forward through the various business channels and is often able to consider the merits of the invention more objectively.

The Inventor as a Product Champion and/or Entrepreneur

Sometimes aninventormay have developed skills or profiles of a product champion and/or entrepreneur.

James Dyson and Thomas Edison are two examples.

Edison (later it was discovered that Swan invented the light bulb) used profits from his earlier inventions to bring the light bulb to market.

15 inventions that changed the world from Edison – Business Insider

James Dyson is an example of an inventor, product champion and/or entrepreneur. He invented the cyclone technology for suction. At first no-one was interested in this radical design so he 'championed' his product until he found a Japanese company would would take it on. Later he would use the profits to further improvements and novel products. He build.an understanding of business.

An article on Dyson

Inventors often take the role of product champion and/or entrepreneur because ...

Their product or idea is novel

Too novel or 'out there' for a company to take a risk on

Cant find a backer or company to produce it

The inventor will have to 'champion' their product to different companies

Edison's Light Bulb – Click for more

Dyson ball-barrow – Click fo 10 of Dysons' machines

A Multidisciplinary Approach to Innovation

On occasion, the inventor is also the product champion and/or entrepreneur.

This requires specific skill sets and actions to fulfil these roles and the reason inventors often take on multiple roles.

Effective design draws from multiple areas of expertise, and this can be utilised at different stages of product development.

Most products are now extremely complex and rely on expertise from various disciplines. Most designs are developed by multidisciplinary teams.

Modern Products such as smart-phones, printer/scanners are very complex.

Requires knowledge from many disciplines.

It would be unlikely that a lone inventor would have the expertise in all the disciplines.

Most modern day designs are developed in multidisciplinary teams

Advantages and Disadvantages of a Multidisciplinary Approach to Innovation.

AdvantagesDisadvantages

wide range of knowledge that others may not have considered

wide range of expertise and/or backgrounds that foster cross-fertilization of ideas

wide range of expertise and/or backgrounds meaning that people look at ideas through a different set of lens

may not want to share ideas for fear of losing ownership

individual may not be use to working in teams

different working styles and speed

chance of miscommunication

Activity: Find and explain how a product or innovation was developed in multidisciplinary teams.

Theory of knowledge

Design favours collective wisdom. Do other areas of knowledge value collaborative thinking?

5.5 PRODUCT LIFE CYCLE

Designers need to consider the whole product cycle of potential products, services and systems throughout the design cycle and beyond. Products may have an impact not only on the direct consumer but also on society at large and the environment.

An understanding of the product life cycle allows the designer to design a product with obsolescence in mind. Doing this at the design stage can potentially eliminate the effect of a product on the environment when it is no longer in use.

Product Life Cycle

Term: Is a tool for mapping out the four stages of a product's commercial life: Launch; Growth; Maturity; Decline.

Product :Life Cycle Chart

IB Product Life Cycle Chart

Key Stages of The Product Life Cycle

Launch: There are slow sales and little profit as the product is launched on the market.

Growth: The market gradually accepts the product, so diffusion starts and sales expand.

Maturity: Sales peak but remain steady, so maximum profit is achieved.

Decline: Market saturation is reached and sales start to reduce as well as profit.

Encyclopedia of Business website on Product Life Cycle

News article on the iPod peaking from – the Sydney Morning Herald

Activity: Find two products that are in each stage of the product life cycle and write a sentence describing why. One product must be new to the market and another a classic design. Put it on Padlet.

Article and image from the SMH

Obsolescence

More longer version is on youtube.

Obsolescence Affects The Product Life Cycle.

Obsolescence is where a product or trend becomes obsolete or outdated and no longer used or needed.

Reason why for many products the product cycle has shortened.

include new safety features.

include latest technology.

trends in fashion or style fluctuate.

ensure a continuing market.

IB has identified 4 types of obsolescence.

Term: Planned Obsolescence – A product becomes outdated as a conscious act either to ensure a continuing market or to ensure that safety factors and new technologies can be incorporated into later versions of the product.

Term: Style (fashion) Obsolescence – Fashions and trends change over time, which can result in a product no longer being desirable. However, as evidenced by the concept of retro styling and the cyclic nature of fashion, products can become desirable again.

Term: Functional Obsolescence – Over time, products wear out and break down. If parts are no longer available, the product can no longer work in the way it originally did. Also, if a service vital to its functioning is no longer available, it can become obsolete.

Term: Technological Obsolescence – When a new technology supersedes an existing technology, the existing technology quickly falls out of use and is no longer incorporated into new products. Consumers instead opt for the newer, more efficient technology in their products.

Planned – Light bulbs – are planned to last a certain mount of hours. Read More.

Activity: Find one example of a product for each of the types of obsolescence.

Activity: Identify and describe one product (other than computers, phones, tablets or MP3 players) that have a shortened product cycle.

Activity: Compare a laptop computer and a ballpoint pen.

Laptop computers are an intensely competitive market, with size and power being key issues. Whereas ball point pens meet the needs of the target market and still sell strongly.

Predictability of The Product Life Cycle

Length of the product life cycle considering the effect of technical development

Length of the product life cycle considering the effect of consumer trends including fashion – unpredictable

Planned is predictable

Product Versioning/Generations

Product Versioning is offering a range of products based on a core or initial product market segments.

A company can maintain a pioneering strategy and consistent revenue flow by introducing new versions or generations of a product to a market. Apple uses this strategy effectively, creating multiple versions and generations of their iPod®, iPhone® and iPad® products.

Investopesia on versioning and advantages

Advantages and disadvantages for a company of introducing new versions and generations of a product

Improved consumer choice: consumers can choose the version thats suits them.

Improved consumer choice: can choose a budget level such as Quicken tax software

Maximise profits for the company hopefully through increased sales.

International-Mindedness

The transition from a linear to a circular economy in the move towards sustainable societies has major implications for the ideas associated with product life cycle.

Theory of Knowledge

Design considers areas other than man in its thinking. Are other areas of knowledge confined to human influence and values?

5.6 ROGERS' CHARACTERISTICS OF INNOVATION AND CONSUMERS

Rogers' four main elements that influence the spread of new ideas (innovation, communication channels, time and a social system) rely heavily on human capital. The ideas must be widely accepted in order to be self- sustainable. Designers must consider various cultures and communities to predict how, why and at what rate new ideas and technology will be adopted.

By categorizing consumers, the designer can identify particular segments with a market sector to gain feedback. By engaging with these stereotypes, the designer can utilize their experiences with a prototype in order to guide further development.

Diffusion and innovation

Diffusion is the wide acceptance and sale of a product or innovation.

A good article from PSU

The impact of Rogers' characteristics on consumer adoption of an innovation

Rogers' Characteristics from the Open University

The impact of Rogers' characteristics on consumer adoption of an innovation can be considered in terms of:

Relative advantage – is the "the degree to which the innovation is perceived as better than the idea it supersedes. Relative advantage refers to the extent to which the innovation is more productive, efficient, costs less, or improves in some other manner upon existing practices".

An example on the Open Uni

Compatibility – is 'the degree to which the innovation is perceived as being consistent with existing values, past experiences, and needs of potential adopters. An innovation must be considered socially acceptable to be implemented. And some innovations require much time and discussion before they become socially acceptable'.

An example on the Open Uni – the mobile phone.

Complexity (simplicity) – is "the degree to which the innovation is perceived as difficult to understand and use".

An example on the Open Uni – GUI (Graphic User Interface) of the Apple computers allowing users to pint and click and what they can see.

Observability – is "the degree to which the results of the innovation are visible to others. The chances of adoption are greater if folks can easily observe relative advantages of the new technology. In fact, after some adopt, observability can improve the diffusion effect, a critical component of technology transfer".

An example on the Open Uni – Solar panels on roofs.

Trialability – is "the degree to which the innovation may be experimented with on a limited basis. Innovations are easier to adopt if they can be tried out in part, on a temporary basis, or easily dispensed with after trial".

An example on the Open Uni – test driving a car.

Quoted from http://www.soc.iastate.edu/sapp/soc415Diffusion1.html

"In general, innovations that are perceived as having relative advantages, being more compatible, less complex, observable, and trialable will diffuse more rapidly than other innovations.In general, innovations that are perceived as having relative advantages, being more compatible, less complex, observable, and trialable will diffuse more rapidly than other innovations." – Open Uni

Social roots of consumerism

lifestyle

values

identity

Issues for companies in the global marketplace when attempting to satisfy consumer needs in relation to lifestyle, values and identity

The influence of social media on the diffusion of innovation

Consumers can influence diffusion of innovation. When considering the influence of social media in rallying support for boycotting of some products/systems, students can explore the concepts behind organizations such as Kickstarter, Sellaband, Seedrs and CrowdCube, which act as crowd-funding platforms for creative products and projects. They can also examine the role of social networks such as Facebook®, LinkedIn® and Twitter® as methods of raising brand awareness.

The influence of trends and the media on consumer choice

Students will need to consider how consumer choices are influenced by trends and the media, including advertising through magazines, television, radio, sponsorship and outdoor advertising; product placement through film and television; product endorsement; and so on.

Categories of consumers

Customer Characterics

This in relation to how adopt consumers technology:

Innovators (risk takers) – are the first individuals to adopt an innovation. They are willing to take risks.

Early adopters (hedgers) – are the second fastest category to adopt an innovation.

Early majority (waiters) – the third group, tends to take more time to consider adopting new innovations and is inclined to draw from feedback from early adopters before taking the risk of purchasing new products/systems.

Late majority (skeptics) – adopts the innovation after it has been established in the marketplace and is seldom willing to take risks with new innovation.

Laggards (slow pokes) – are the last to adopt an innovation. They tend to prefer traditions and are unwilling to take risks.

International-mindedness:

The origin of Rogers' theory in one or two areas may lead to inappropriate application on a global basis. Positive and negative aspects may be opposite in different regions/countries.

Theory of knowledge:

Design takes into account cultural differences. Are other areas of knowledge universal or culture specific?

5.7 INNOVATION, DESIGN AND MARKETING SPECIFICATIONS

Designers must establish clear parameters for a marketing specification in order to create unique and creative solutions to a problem. Designers need to collect valid and useful data from the target market and audience throughout the design cycle to ensure the specification includes certain essential components.

The ability to transform their research findings into a series of specifications is a skill that designers must develop to become successful. Being able to express parameters and requirements succinctly allows the designer to develop focused solutions to the design problem and meet a client or the target market's wants and needs.

Marketing Specifications

Marketing specifications relate to market and user characteristics of the proposed design and details.

Target markets

When determining the target market, market sectors and segments need to be identified.

How market sectors and segments can be used to establish target markets

Ask yourself: Who is most likely to buy this product given its benefits? How can the organization tap into the buying power of these consumers? Where is the target market most likely to find out about the product? Answering these questions helps you to position your product in the correct marketing and distribution channels.

Target audiences

It is important to differentiate between the target market and the target audience. When determining the target audience, characteristics of the users should be established.

How a target audience is used to establish the characteristics of users

Market analysis

An appraisal of economic viability of the proposed design from a market perspective, taking into account fixed and variable costs and pricing, is important. It is typically a summary about potential users and the market.

User need

A marketing specification should identify the essential requirements that the product must satisfy in relation to market and user need.

Competition

A thorough analysis of competing designs is required to establish the market need.

Every product you take to market, even ones that are new inventions or improvements on old products, face competition. This is because customers buy products for many different reasons. Some are interested in the innovation of new products, others care more about price point and clever marketing schemes. Your competition will capitalize on these buyer preferences and seek to edge out your product from the market. Identifying the competition in your marketing specification helps the organization to clarify how it can edge out and respond to the competition.

Research methods

Consider design contexts for different target markets and audiences

This will govern the type os research method you will use

Topic 9.4 has a list of possible research strategies/methods

Design Specifications

A design specification relates to the requirements of a product and details aspects of:

aesthetic requirements

cost constraints

customer requirements

environmental requirements

size constraints

safety considerations

performance requirements and constraints

materials requirements

manufacturing requirements.

any others that pertain to the design context

All of the requirements, constraints and considerations must be specific, feasible and measurable.

The design specification must be developed from the design brief and research.

International-mindedness:

The characteristics of users in different countries/regions need to be taken into account. Cultural differences may play a major role.

Theory of knowledge:

Design is evidence-based. How do other areas of knowledge value the importance of evidence?

CHAPTER SIX

Classic Design

6.1 CHARACTERISTICS OF CLASSIC DESIGN

A classic design is not simply defined by how well it functions or its impact. Classic designs can be recognized as from their design movement/era. Yet, originality— whether it is evolutionary or revolutionary—seems to be the trait that makes a product "timeless".The iconic status of classic designs is often attributed to them being 'breakthrough products'.

Term: Design Classic – A product that serves as a standard of its time, that has been manufactured industrially and has timeless appeal.

Regardless in what year or time period it still remains at a high standard.

A classic design is instantly recognisable and will provoke

Vespa 98 – Visit the History of the Vespa

different emotional responses.

These could include: desire to need or want it, 'wow' factor (innovation), nostalgia, 'like' or 'hate', etc

Often referred to as "iconic",the longevity of classic designs suggests quality,

Levi's 501 Visit the history of Levi's

the continued demand for such products is not dependent on heavy marketing or advertising,

although this often takes place to reinforce the status and remind new generations of consumers of the intrinsic value of the classic design.

The design is often widely imitated, usually with cheaper versions,

so this reinforces the status of the original design and its "pioneering" concept.

The classic design may no longer be needed as a functional object or it may become technologically obsolete.

However, it may still sell very small numbers although it may no longer be viable to produce it commercially.

In such circumstances the resale value of existing products increases enormously as the number of products available lessens over time.

Such products become very collectable

$6000 Matchbox Car – Visit the Matchbox Car Museum

and have investment value, for example, classic cars.

Other products may not intrinsically be worth much money but are valuable to certain owners or collectors, such as toys that have been used and are in poor condition.

For many centuries prior to the Industrial Revolution, "classic" evoked thoughts of artistry and craft skills, for example, classical architecture and furniture. The advent of mass production and "designing for the masses" often meant a reduction in quality of products and poor design. However, once mass production techniques became more established some designers embraced the opportunities offered by the new techniques and materials as a way of providing people with well-designed products at an affordable price due to the cost-effectiveness of production. No longer was classic design the preserve of the elite in society.

The Design Museum has a good coverage of designers and designs that have shaped our lives.

British Post celebrates 'British Classic and Iconic Designs'

50 Iconic designs

Characteristics of a Classic Design

Image

Term: Within the context of classic design, image relates to the instantly recognizable aesthetics of a particular product. For example, the shape of a Coca-Cola bottle, or the shape of a Volkswagen Beetle motor car.

Image makes a classic design instantly recognisable and provokes emotional reactions

highly recognisable aesthetics

representation of an external form

evokes emotional attachment

Coke bottles in different languages

VW Beetle

Status

Term: Products considered as classic designs often increase in value and can project a certain status as they become more desirable. The ownership of a classic design can increase the perceived status of an individual.

A classic design can indicate the status (social position) of an individual.

Increase in the perceived status of a person.

Connections with the elite class

Conveys a feeling of satisfaction.

A feeling of owning a rarity.

Ferrari

Culture

Term: In the context of classic design, culture plays an important part. They often reflect cultural influences and mark transition points within a particular culture. The culture of concern may be national, religious or a sub-culture, such as a particular youth culture or movement.

Design classics can reflect cultural influences.

It may be a national or religious cultural influence.

Vegemite is strongly associated with Australia. Even the advertising Jingle is a cultural icon.

It may concern a sub-culture such as a particular youth culture or movement.

For example UK Skinheads' footwear were Dr Martens boots with its yellow stitching.

Evokes emotional attachment

Nostalgia

A sense of belonging

What first comes to mind when you see Vegemite?

Dr Martens

Obsolescence

Term: This is the stage in a product life cycle where the product is no longer needed even though it functions as well as it did when first manufactured. Classic designs tend to transcend obsolescence and become desired objects long after they have ceased to be manufactured.

Obsolescence is something becoming obsolete or of no longer any use. Consumer electronics such as your mobile phone often fall into this category. Many people will replace there mobile within a few years.

A classic design defies (transcend) obsolescence.

It is timeless

It is still a desired object long after they have ceased to be manufactured.

A classic design transcends (goes beyond) its original function.

Its unchanging (or minutely changed) design spans time.

Mass production

Mass production contributes to a product reaching classic design status such as the VW shown below or the Bic Pen.

being mass-produced spanning decades leads to it being ever present or omnipresent.

Mass-production made cars affordable (due to economies of scale) so it sold well.

Mass-production made them easily available.

Its simple design (and mechanics) lent itself to mass production.

VW Beetle vs Transporter

Ubiquitous/Omnipresence

Term: Omnipresence – In the context of classic design, a product that is omnipresent has existed and been in circulation for a long time.

Term: Ubiquitous – In the context of classic design, a product that is ubiquitous is one that can be found almost everywhere. For example, a mobile phone.

A classic design often has a constant presence, or omnipresence, in a rapidly changing context and has been in constant circulation.

Ball point pens

Dominant Design

Term: The design contains those implicit features of a product that are recognized as essential by a majority of manufacturers and purchasers.

For example Coca-cola – the shape of the bottle, the font and red colour.

Classic designs that are also dominant designs in the marketplace are difficult to change them.

because it is popular or omni-presencent

those that have defied obsolescence and have been a round a long time tend to have emotional attachments

Nostalgia

Dominant design has been around a while, if it changes not so recognisable and the company could risk profits

The "QWERTY" keyboard layout was specifically designed (to make people inefficient) to replace the flaws of the mechanical typewriter by changing the order of the letters on the keyboard. Now it is recognised as well used worldwide and preferred over the more logical and formal keyboard layouts. By the way, did you know that you can type faster one handed than on a QWERTY keyboard.

Coca Cola

Activity

Choose two products that you consider to be classic designs.

Write a sentence or two why you consider it to be classic.

Include an image.

Add it to the Padlet "Classic Designs"

Look the ToK and IM statements below.

Find a classic design that you think that evokes an emotion in one culture but maybe not in another culture or in the same culture.

Include an image.

Write a sentence why.

Add it to the Padlet "Classic Design and emotions"

International Mindedness:

Classic designs are often recognized across culture and hold iconic status.

Theory of Knowledge:

Classic design often appeals to our emotions. Are emotions universal?

6.2 CLASSIC DESIGN, FUNCTION AND FORM

Classic design holds "form follows function" as a fundamental principle, but this is not always evident in practice. Some products are so well designed with function as their primary goal, that their use is intuitive. As designers develop new technologies, the lines between the form and function of a product continue to blur.

The balance between function and form is often an area of difficulty for the designer. If a product is purely functional, it may be lacking in appeal to consumers, no matter how good it may be at completing its job. Often we are drawn to products that have been developed with form as a primary consideration. The human psyche appreciates beauty.

Classic designs are harmonious, well-proportioned in form and often restrained in style. To reinterpret a classic design, the original form needs to be respected and the underlying structure of the form understood before making changes. Decoration applied must be suitable for the form and take into account the function of the object, although "classic" does not necessarily mean the style needs to be minimalist in nature or lacking in decoration.

Form versus function

Term: Form – Also considered as the three-dimensional space that a product takes up, in the context of classic design, form relates to the shape of a product and the aesthetic qualities that the shape gives.

Term: Function – Products can be considered classic designs based on how well they fulfil the task that they have been designed for.

Not all classic designs are based on form or aesthetics as a main reason for the design or product.

For example, the designers of many early examples of mass production motor cars that are now considered "classics" were more interested in function than form.

The Volkswagen (VW) Beetle, designed by Ferdinand Porsche in the 1930s, was aimed at ordinary people with a modest income and Porsche economized on many features considered as standard and necessary today, such as a rear window.

Alec Issigonis designed the first Mini motor car to be as economical and functional as possible and priced so it was affordable by the majority of working people in the late 1950s.

1936 Beetle

2010 Beetle

1950's Mini Cooper

2018 Mini Cooper

Activity: Compare the original production models of the VW beetle, BMW or the Mini cars with their more modern day versions. Consider form verses function. Go to the Padlet.

Practical Function versus Psychological Function

The tension between form and function when developing new products based on a classic design

Practical function is mostly concerned with criteria related to the performance of the product, such as dimensions, weight, ease of use, etc.

These are quantifiable and as a result an objective evaluation can be carried out. (Quantitative data)

Anglepoise lamp design by George Carwardine (an UK engineer) in 1947 is an example where practical function is of a primary concern over form.

Carwardine was interested in an apparatus that could move easily through three planes but would be rigid when left free. It was many years before Carwardine worked on this concept as a versatile "arm" for focusing light on an object. Although Carwardine made no particular effort to make his lamp an object of beauty, its clean and functional form has established the Anglepoise lamp as a design classic.

Psychological function is mostly concerned with the different emotional reactions or attachments people have with products such as mobile phones or their favourite piece of apparel.

These are subjective criteria. (qualitative data)

The Juicy Salif lemon squeezer, designed by Philip Starck in 1990 and produced by the Italian company Alessi, is an example of how the psychological function dictates the form of an object. The design was conceived on a napkin while Starck enjoyed a dish of squid in a restaurant and was squeezing lemon over it. Starck is quoted as saying that his juicer is less concerned with squeezing lemons than as a conversation starter. An example of Starck's lemon squeezer is on display in the New York Museum of Modern Art.

The way in which humans need to interact with objects often dictates their form. This interaction may be classified into three aspects:

assembling the object either during manufacture or at home (self-assembly)

using it

repairing or maintaining it.

For example, when designing mobile phones the success of the human-interaction interface is important, there, a compromise of function over form, in this case.

Anglepoise Lamp

Juicy Salif Lemon Squeezr

Conflict and Compromise

Conflict and compromise can occur during the development of the product.

Teams of specialists comprising of ergonomists, electrical engineers, materials engineers and product designers are involved in the development of industrial designed products.

Form over function may be an important aspect of the design for some members while for others it maybe function over form.

When considering form, students need to understand how it can be dictated by other functions such as design for manufacture techniques, for example, design for disassembly.

"Designers traditionally find themselves trying to perform a balancing act between conflicting design parameters; weight versus strength, speed versus life, efficiency versus complexity, or efficiency versus cost, to name but a few common trade-off scenarios" from The TRZ Journal

Activity: Practical than Psychological

Identify one product that is more practical than psychological in function.

Identify one product that is more practical than psychological in function.

Post a picture and one sentence why for each on the Padlet

Retro-Styling

Term: A design that uses the form and decoration from a particular period of time and/or style.

A Wikipedia reference.

A Retro-styled product uses a classic image with modern-day technologies.

The 'Roberts' digital radio (shown below) is based on the style of old transistor radios is an example.

Retro-styling a new product needs to respect and understand the original form and underlying structure before making changes

The Kombi is back!

Roberts Digital Radio

Vintage Roberts Radio

Art Deco (Retro-Styling)

Art Deco Style (1930's) has its roots form the exclusive hand-made French decorative arts (1920's).

It became incredibly popular decades later due to mass production (economies of scale) of products using different materials, such as metals, plastic and glass.

Being a decorative style it was easily added to many products (lamps, furniture) or surfaces (e.g. buildings)

It was used widely in Architecture and lighting.

1920's Art Deco Lamp

Art Deco Furniture

International Mindedness

The emergence of retro-styling products as new technologies are developed relate to the emotional response that comes with nostalgia. This is often not only different between countries and between generations, but at the same time can transcend both.

Theory of knowledge

Is aesthetic value purely a subjective matter?

CHAPTER SEVEN

User Centred Design (UCD)

7.1 USER-CENTRED DESIGN (UCD)

A designer must consider the needs, wants and limitations of the end user within every element ofthe design cycle. The ability to identify how users will interact with a product, service or system is vital forits success. To achieve this, designers must be able to acquire and analyse valid data without making assumptions about how the product may be used.

The ability to put aside one's own ideas and bias is essential for UCD. Designers must act with integrity and not project their own ideas of what the user requirements are when trying to create technological solutions to their problems.

The Designer Needs to Have a Deep Understanding of the User, Task and the Environment.

Donald Norman (who developed the concept) found that products:

were difficult to use.

often included style changes solely for style sake which reduced usability.

these inclusions increased the cost.

increased complexity.

reduction in efficient use.

The principles of UCD to the design process.

A design is based upon an explicit understanding of users, tasks and environments.

Users are involved throughout design and development.

The design is driven and refined by user-centred evaluation.

The process is iterative.

The design addresses the whole user experience.

The design team includes multidisciplinary skills and perspectives, such as Don Norman's engineering and psychology degrees.

Students should be able to apply the above.

User-Centered Design and the User, Task & Environment

Term: UCD is a design process paying particular attention to the needs of potential users of a product through involvement of users at all stages of the design process.

Term: Empathetic – When the designer takes the place of the user to see who potentially could use the product and the object could be better suited for the consumer.

The Uncomfortable web site – non UCD

User-Centered Design and the UserUser-Centered Design and the TaskUser-Centered Design and the Environment

Term: User – Person utilising the product, person who is being affected by the product or who is reaping benefits/drawbacks.Term: Task – The thing that the product is supposed to do, however the user may have several sub uses for the product.Term: Environment – The place where a product is likely to be used.

It considers how users are likely to use the product and tests products with actual users.

Sometimes called "empathic design", the user-centred approach puts the design team in direct contact with the people they are designing for, that is, to empathize with potential users and so gain a better understanding of users' thoughts, needs, values and beliefs.

Often functionality can be included easily and cheaply into a design but too many can reduce it usability.

Electronic interfaces such has TV or satellite remotes is a good example where the complex functionality is too much to understand for most consumers.

Takes into account common tasks such as ticketing vending machines, ATM or a stove top need special consideration

The interface should be a standard that is the user goes from stove top to another or different Bank ATM's it is easily understood and can perform the task easily and efficiently

Important functions are easily recognised.

Takes into account in the use of a product in a particular environment.

Environments like open plan office, car or kitchen (working envelope).

Car: location and layout of controls promote efficiency and safety while driving

car window controls on the door

stereo controls on the steering wheel

blue tooth control over the secondary functions in the car

A baffling Remote

ATM User Interface

VW steering wheel controls

The Process is Iterative, Led by the User and Developed Through User-Centred Evaluation

Term: Iterative – Act of repeating a process with the aim of approaching a desired goal, target or result. Each repetition of the process is also called an iteration, and the results of one iteration are used as the starting point for the next iteration.

UCD is iterative just like the design cycle. Here though emphasis is on the user throughout the product design cycle. At each stage the user is consulted and modifications are made until the consumer requirements are met. Then it is released. See below the Five Stages of UCD

The Five Stages of UCD

User-centred design model from IB TSM

Research

Business and User problems and requirements are analysed.

The user, task and environment are considered

This can be done with a multi-disciplinary teams of ethnographer, anthropologists and psychologists

NB the above diagram for Research

Concept

Initial ideas are put forward

Concept modelling takes place, including paper models

Allows for tactile and appearance evaluations

Evaluation is fed back into the design cycle

It is quick and cheap to carry out.

A multi-disciplinary team of designers, various engineers and psychologists.

NB the above diagram for Concept

Design

Development of ideas

Scaled models such as prototypes, mock ups etc are made

Monitoring of performance against usability requirements

Allows for more continued evaluation by the user and design team.

Evaluation is fed back into the design cycle

NB the above diagram for Design

Implementation

Various testing and evaluations are carried out with a wide range of end users

Evaluation is fed back into the design cycle

A multi-disciplinary team is used to measure the end-users psychological and physiological experience.

NB the above diagram for Implementation

Launch

The end product is launched

Continuos evaluation is carried out

Monitoring of performance against usability requirements

NB the above diagram for Launch

UCD Design Teams are Multidisciplinary.

As can be seen from the five stages of UCD that many other experts are used in the design and production of a UCD product.

These include: anthropologists (study humans, human behaviors and society), ethnographers (study in people and cultures), engineers (deal with the built environment), psychologists (study of the mind) and focus groups to advise the creative designers.

Inclusive Design

Term: The design of mainstream products and/or services so that they are accessible and usable by as many people as possible without the need for adaptation or specialised design.

UCD is a part of Inclusive design. Inclusive design is about designing universally accessible products for all users regardless of age, physical, sensory, perceptual functioning levels (disability). By designing products for all users regardless ability will ensure there is a market for their products and increases their feasibility as an innovation.

Inclusive design is:

Welcoming to everyone

Responsive to people's needs

Intuitive to use

Flexible

Convenient so they can be used without undue effort or special separation and so that they maximise independence

The design council on Inclusive design (the video above)

Inclusive Design

The Product Must Address the Whole User Experience.

Term: User Experience – A person's perceptions and responses that result from the use or anticipated use of a product, system or service, this can modify over time due to changing usage circumstances.

UCD answers questions about users and their tasks and goals, then uses the findings to make decisions about development and design.

Who are the users of the product?

What are the users' tasks and goals?

What are the users' experiences and expertise with the product and products like it?

What functionality do the users require of the product?

What other stakeholders will be impacted by the product?

Why is the product being developed?

What are the overall objectives?

How will the product be used?

How will it be judged a success?

What are the technical and environmental constraints?

What functionality is needed by users?

What are the typical scenarios of how and why users will use the product?

What are the usability goals?

How important is ease of use and ease of learning?

How long should it take users to complete their tasks?

Is it important to minimize user errors?

Are there any initial design concepts?

International Mindedness

Even though the task addressed through UCD may not change from region to region, there can be an impact on the success of a global product due to variations in users and environments.

7.2 USABILITY

A design team should be "user" driven and frequent contact with potential users is essential. To understand how a product, service or system may be used, the designer must consider the prior knowledge and experience of the users, as well as their typical psychological responses. Evaluation methods that utilize appropriate testing and trialling strategies must be used to determine these aspects

Designers must consider the limits of population stereotypes. Through recognizing these limits, the designers can critically assess the appropriateness of their product in relation to those who will use it.

Usability is how well a human-made product (tool, machine, webpage, a system or process) can be effectively (completely and accurately) and efficiently (fast and with minimum effort) used by users.

It functions in a predictable and consistent way.

The human-made product can be considered intuitive, pleasant, enjoyable to use, prevents user errors or if errors occur then the user can easily recover.

From the ISO ... Usability is concerned with "the extent to which a product can be used by specified users to achieve specified goals with effectiveness, efficiency and satisfaction in a specified context of use" (ISO 9241-11, 1998)

Usability objectives

Usefulness

Once users have learned the design, how quickly can they perform tasks?

Efficiently – fast and with minimum effort

Effectiveness

Use the design completely and accurately

Prevents errors

User can recover if errors occur.

Learnability

It is the ease at which the user can learn to use a product?

The intuitiveness to use a product, service or system design.

How easy is it for users to accomplish tasks the first time they encounter the design?

Memorable – when the user returns they do not have to re-learn how to use it.

Attitude

Satisfaction or likability when the client uses or interacts with the product, service or system design.

How pleasant is it to use the design?

Enhanced usability

Benefits of enhanced usability include:

improved product acceptance

improved user experience

improved productivity

reduces user error

reduces the need for training and support

Characteristics of good user-product interfaces

Characteristics of good user-product interfaces (is the space where a user and machine interact) include:

Simplicity – simple design allows for clarity on how the design can be used such as an iPod interface.

Ease of use – iPod interface has limited menu items that are easily and quickly accessed.

Intuitive logic and organization – Novice users of a product should be able to learn all its basic functions within one or two hours.

However, many products are full of confusing detail and are difficult to learn. This can lead to incomplete use of the product's functionality and frustration for the user.

Instruction manuals are often poorly written and poorly organized.

It is difficult for the designer of a product to distance him/herself from the product and look at it through the eyes of the prospective user. Reinnovation of a product often involves adding features to the basic design rather than redesigning the user–product interface from scratch, and this can result in a disorganized interface. It is important to consider necessary

and desirable features, not ones that increase complexity without enhancing usefulness for most users.

Low memory burden – the user does not need to have to memorise many features, how to use it, etc.

Do not have to relearn functions. Poor organization of a product imposes a memory burden on users, who have to learn and remember how the various functions work.

This results in them not using the full functionality of a product but focusing on a limited set of features and ignoring those that are difficult to remember.

Thinking about how intuitively the product features can be accessed by users can reduce memory burden and make the product more user-friendly.

Visibility – Controls should be visible and it should be obvious how they work.

They should convey the correct message, for example, with doors that need to be pushed, the designer must provide signals that indicate where to push.

Feedback – Feedback is the provision of information, for example, an audible tone to a user, as a result of an action.

The tone on a telephone touchpad or the click of a key on a computer keyboard provides feedback to indicate that a key has been pressed.

The "egg timer" icon on a computer screen tells the user that an action is being undertaken.

Affordance – Affordance is the property of an object that indicates how it can be used.

Buttons afford pushing, and knobs afford turning.

On a door, handles afford pulling, whereas push plates afford pushing.

Consider how the use of a handle on a door that needs to be pushed open can confuse users, and how in an emergency this might impact on safety considerations.

Mapping – Mapping relates to the correspondence between the layout of the controls and their required action.

For example, the layout of the controls on a cooker hob can take advantage of physical analogies and cultural standards to facilitate a user's understanding of how it works.

Constraints – Constraints limit the way that a product can be used.

The design of a three-pin plug or a USB (universal serial bus) device ensures that they are inserted the correct way.

This reduces or eliminates the possibility of a user making errors.

The user–product interfaces of many electronic products are extremely complex rather than being intuitive and easy to use. Products with intuitive and easily accessible interfaces are likely to be more popular with consumers.

Population stereotypes

A stereotype is when a person is catorgerised into a population based on culture, class, gender, etc. This allows assumptions and associations on how that particular stereotyped population may, react in a situation, dress, use of products, aesthetics, values and so on.

White is Western culture symbolizes, purity, elegance and peace. Brides often where white wedding gowns. In Asian cultures white represents, death, mourning or bad luck. Traditionally white is worn at funerals.

A short list of different traditional wedding dress colors.

This has implications on color selection and aesthetics.

In Australia and China, to turn a light switch it is flipped down. In the USA it is flipped up.

This has implications of standardization of products.

In Australia and China the difference int he orientation of a 3 pin electrical wall socket is another example.

Chinese Wedding Dress

Western Wedding Gown

Chinese Wall Socket

Australian Wall Socket

Advantages and disadvantages of using population stereotypes for designers and users.

Advantages:

Allows you to form assumptions and associations about of a group of people. D

Judgements and decisions can be made quickly. D

Possibly predict the behavior or possible use of a product or system. D & U

The user needs and behavior can be identified and thus usability considerations are met. U

Disadvantages:

Assumptions and associations of a particular stereotype may not fit all people of that population. D

Judgements and decisions could be incorrect. D

Not all people who 'look alike act/think alike' there fore behavior or way a product was intended to be used may be wrong. U & D

International Mindedness

Population stereotypes based on cultural expectations contribute to human error and designers must consider this when designing good user-product interfaces.

At the beginning of this video he makes mention of global designing.

Sample Questions

Identify three characteristics of good user–product interfaces.

Explain the disadvantages of user–product interfaces that are not well organized and cannot be learnt intuitively and remembered easily.

Discuss the impact of memory burden on the user-friendliness of a product.

Explain why it is difficult for designers to develop simple intuitive user–product interfaces.

7.3 STRATEGIES FOR USER RESEARCH

Designers should select research strategies based on the desired user experiences in the context of the product, service or system. The purpose of user research is to identify needs that reveal the complexities of personae. Real-life scenarios that simulate "actual" user experiences can generate new findings.

The various strategies for user research can be used by the designer to explore the true nature of a problem. Through the use of personae and use cases, the designer can build a range of possible scenarios with which to explore the problem in detail.

User population

User population is a range of users for a particular product or system.

A product maybe design for a particular population.

Easy grip can opener for people with arthritis

On the other hand, some products can be designed for use by different or multiple populations.

When considering strategies for user research, designers need to consider their appropriateness in relation to user populations.

Classification of users

People of user populations are classified into groups based on age, gender and physical condition.

physical conditions may include mobility issues, amputees, blindness, arthritis and so on.

This can allow the designer to gather detailed feedback to generate insights for design development that are particular to each group.

For example, a group of users who suffer from arthritis in their wrists would have different concerns with the design of a new kettle and give different feedback than a population of students.

Another example is IDEO's project in designing homes for wounded war veterans.

The use of personae

Designers can observe and interview members of a user population in order to create fictional characters known as personae, secondary personae and anti-personae.

Personae are the primary target audience they are the 'typical' stakeholder.

Secondary personae are not the primary target audience for a product, but whose needs the product should meet.

They provide valuable 'alternative' insights to the development of a product.

Anti-personae are those for whom the product is not designed.

Personas are used to collect data to better understand the market.

Blog by an app designer

Wikipedia reference on Persona (User Centered Design)

Design of Business seats with EADS using persona

Scenarios

Scenarios offer a physical and social context for different personae

A scenario is an imagined sequence of events in the daily life of a persona based on assumptions by researchers and designers.

Scenarios are based on best, worst and average case. Imagining any conceivable situation.

Students need to be able to consider best-, worst- and average-case scenarios that provide a physical and social context for different personae.

Use case

A set of possible sequences of interactions or event steps between a user and a product to achieve a particular action.

It depict all possible interactions

Can be shown in step form or in a diagram

Use case sample on this website

ATM Use Case

Use Case Diagram

International-mindedness:

User population behaviours, wants and needs may vary from one community of potential users to another, which may result in the development of a product family.

Theory of knowledge:

Design considers the needs of individuals as paramount. Is this the case in other areas of knowledge?

7.4 STRATEGIES FOR USER-CENTRED DESIGN (UCD)

For designers to successfully integrate usability into the design process, they require a holistic understanding of how a product, service or system is used. Designers must identify user requirements through the use of careful observation and interviews. A clear strategy for UCD will improve acceptability and usability, reducing costs and effort, while fulfilling user requirements.

By including potential consumers in the testing of designs and prototypes, designers gain valuable data relating to how they will interact with a product.

The strategies for UCD:

DesignKit has a good explanation and case studies

Field research

A first hand observation of customer's user experience.

It is essential for the research to be conducted in the user's environment.

These can be field trials, ethnographic interviews or observations in the real world

AdvantagesDisadvantages

Gain first hand knowledge

Gain first hand experience

Obtain detailed data of people and processes

It emphasizes the role and relevance of social context.

Data will be very narrow

emotional taxing as relationship between interviewer and client has to be established.

Method of extremes

A common sampling method where users are selected to represent the extremes of a user population, typically the 2.5th and 97.5th percentile.

Products are then designed and/or tested to ensure that they function efficiently for those users.

Design equipment for general use

Another explanation from DesignKit

A an interesting blog post

Slideshow on Extremes

AdvantagesDisadvantages

greatest number of users are accommodated

maybe sensitive for extreme groups to be involved

Observation

Essentially is a user trial where the intended client uses the product and the expert observes.

This can be in the field (natural environment) or in a lab (controlled environment)

AdvantagesDisadvantages

Help to unveil usability issues

Tested under conditions of use

Data collected maybe difficult to analyse

Interviews and Focus groups

A collection of responses from users, a trail of observation of users interacting with the product

AdvantagesDisadvantages

It is dynamic

Face to Face

Body language and gestures can be observed

Easily measure reactions

Clarifying questions can be asked

Expensive as interviewees are often compensated

Participants may not wish to share sensitive issues

Small sample size may not be truly representative of the whole

Moderator bias

Questionnaires

A series of questions to solicit information

AdvantagesDisadvantages

Cheap

Easy to administer

large numbers of questionnaires can be administered

sent easily to a wide local, national, global regions

Static

poor number of responses

maybe only interested people fill out the survey thus perhaps a bias

Affinity diagramming

A graphical tool that identifies a general theme to collect facts, opinions and ideas.

They express data and infromation in a common format by creating clusters and groups of common information.

It represents a text based map which shows aspects of the product that has been/will be taken into consideration in the design and manufacturing of the product, thereby presenting the results.

Usability.net of affinity diagrams

AdvantagesDisadvantages

Simple

Cost effective

Easy to get data from a group

builds teamwork

time consuming

can get quite large

Participatory design, prototype and usability testing session.

Participatory design is an approach to design attempting to actively involve all stakeholders (e.g. employees, partners, customers, citizens, end users) in the design process to help ensure the result meets their needs and is usable. (Wikipedia)

An example of participatory design is when users representing the target market for a product perform realistic tasks by interacting with a paper version of the user-product interface manipulated by a person acting as a computer who does not explain how the interface works.

Prototype see Topic 3 on modelling

Usability testing is carried out in a usability laboratory. Typically, users are seated with an instructor who observes them performing a particular task with the product. Another group of observers is behind a one-way mirror, where they can record the activity and note insights. Often the tests are recorded for later reference and analysis.

Natural environments and usability laboratories

Natural environments Usability laboratories

The potential client is observed using the product, system or service where it is intended to be used

Advantage: solicit data from real and intended contexts

Advantage: usability is tested in the intended environment

Disadvantage: biased opinions from the observers

Disadvantage: mostly qualitative data is collected.

The potential client is observed using the product, system or service in a controlled.

Advantage: controlled environment can ensure that product/service/system is used as intended.

Advantage: Groups of 'observers' can view the usability and a more wider view of analysis

Advantage: labs can be set up with high-tech sensors and equipment for better monitoring.

Disadvantage: can be costly as facilities/personnel must be hired.

Disadvantage: can be intimidating to know people are behind one-way mirrors

Testing houses versus usability laboratories

There are many advantages and disadvantages between using natural environments and usability laboratories and between using usability laboratories and testing houses for design companies.

International Mindedness

Testing in the environment where a product will be used is often extremely important for the design of products, especially where the problem to solve occurs in a country foreign to the design team.

Theory of Knowledge

Is it ever possible to eliminate the effect of the observer?

To what extent does the language used on questionnaires shape the results?

7.5 BEYOND USABILITY—DESIGNING FOR PLEASURE AND EMOTION

A designer's ability to provide satisfaction through aesthetic appeal and pleasure can greatly influence the success of a product, service or system. Understanding attitudes, expectations and motivations of consumers plays a significant role in predicting product interaction. Designers need to be empathetic and sympathetic to user emotion, which acts as a critical component to determine how he or she interprets and interacts with a product, service or system.

The ability to express emotion through a product can not only build appeal for the consumer, but also build affinity between a product and consumer. It can enable a product to communicate how one should interact with it.

Why Design for Pleasure/Emotion

Online book from ScienceDirect on Design for Emotion.

Attitude: The perceptions, feelings and opinions about a product by a user.

We want to create products that people love.

To make it a pleasure to use – reduce complexity – it's usable!

People become 'attached' to a product

Engage the user/consumer in the product

This will also develop brand loyalty

if a consumer is satisfied with the product, they'll come back

Increase or maintain sales for a company

and Mr T says 'its just nice' (don't write this bullet on your exam)

The four-pleasure framework

The four-pleasure framework was identified by Professor Lionel Tiger from Rutgers University in New Jersey, USA. It includes the following areas.

Socio-pleasure

Is derived from social interaction.

Products and services can facilitate social interaction in a number of ways.

Examples include:

Email, internet and mobile phones that facilitate communication between people.

Products may promote social interaction by being conversation starters, for example, jewelry, artwork or furniture.

Clothing can communicate social identity and indicate that a person belongs to a particular social group.

Physio-pleasure

Is derived from the feel of a product during use

Examples include:

wearing a silk garment or the smooth feel of an iPod/iPhone,

taste such as eating chocolate

smell of leather, a new car, coffee or freshly baked bread

Psycho-pleasure

Is derived from the cognitive demands of using a product or service and the emotional reactions engendered through the experience of using it.

The outcome may also be more emotionally satisfying and less stressful.

Examples include:

it might be expected that a word processor that facilitated quick and easy accomplishment of tasks would provide a higher level of psycho-pleasure than one with which the user was likely to make many errors. The former word processor should enable the user to complete the task more easily than he or she would with the latter.

Ideo-pleasure

Is derived from products that are aesthetically pleasing by appealing to the consumer's values.

Values could be philosophical or religious or may relate to some particular issue such as the environment or a political movement.

These values can be embodied in products.

Examples include:

A product made from biodegradable materials might be seen as embodying the value of environmental responsibility.

Design for emotion

Designing for emotion can increase:

User engagement

Product or brand loyalty

Satisfaction with a product by incorporating emotion and personality

Visceral design: Design that speaks to people's nature in terms of how they expect products and systems to function and how they expect to interact with them.

Reflective Design: Design that evokes personal memory focussing on the message, culture and the meaning of a product or its use.

Behavioural design: Focussed on use and understanding, this considers how people will use a product, focussing on functionality.

This is a good website going into more depth from Usabilla.

Design for Emotion

What is design ..

The attract/converse/transact (ACT) model

How the ACT model can be used as a framework for creating designs that intentionally trigger positive emotional responses

Attract/Converse/Transact (ACT) model (Van Gorp, Adams 2012)* is a framework for creating designs that improve the relations of users with a product and intentionally trigger emotional responses.

The attract part of the model is aesthetics oriented.

The converse part of the model is interaction oriented.

The transact part of the model is function oriented.

ACT Model

ACT Model

When all three elements are addressed, products can become desirable, usable and useful.

*Van Gorp, T and Adams, E. 2012. Design for Emotion. Waltham, Massachusetts, USA. Morgan Kaufman.

Theory of Knowledge

Are emotions purely physiological or are they culturally bound?

CHAPTER EIGHT

Sustainability

8.1 SUSTAINABLE DEVELOPMENT

Designers utilize design approaches that support sustainable development across a variety of contexts. A holistic and systematic approach is needed atall stages of design development to satisfy all stakeholders. In order to develop sustainable products, designers must balance aesthetic, cost, social, cultural, energy, material, health and usability considerations.

Triple bottom line sustainability does not only focus on the profitability of an organization or product, but also the environmental and social benefit it can bring.

Organizations that embrace triple bottom line sustainability can make significant positive effects to the lives of others and the environment by changing the impact of their business activities.

Sustainable DevelopmentSustainability

Sustainability & Sustainable Development

Term: Sustainability is the long-term maintenance of responsibility, which has environmental, economic and social dimensions. It is the capacity to endure and maintain.

Autodesk, Coca cola and McDonald's approach to Sustainability.

Term: Sustainable Development meets the needs of the present without compromising the ability of future generations to meet their own needs.

Triple Bottom Line Sustainability

Term: An expanded spectrum of values and criteria for measuring organizational success: economic, environmental and social.

From IB

TBL

Environmental Aspect of TBL

It is technically possible to deliver the same or equivalent goods and services with lower environmental impact while maintaining social and equity benefits.

Is involved in maintaining the ecosystem by optimising (using) its resources more prudently.

This could include redesigning production system to be more efficient.

Maintaining ecosystem integrity

Assess and work within the carrying capacity (the size of a population that an ecosystem can support without degradation of social, economic and environmental systems).

Recognising and maintaining biodiversity.

Historically there has been a close correlation between economic growth and environmental degradation—as economic prosperity increases so environmental quality decreases.

This trend is clearly demonstrated on graphs of human population numbers, economic growth and environmental indicators, see graph below.

Sustainable development frameworks enable the evaluation of the complex and interrelated concepts that are associated with development.

Correlation graph

CO2 Emissions vs GDP

Social Aspect of TBL

There is a correlation between economic development and human well-being.

See graph below.

International Development on Wikipedia. It mentions economics influence.

Social sustainability:

Designing to develop goods and services for the enhancement of human well-being,

maintaining cultural identity,

empowerment of local communities,

accessibility to resources and services,

stability of communities not placing them in upheaval

social and gender equity

GDP vs Social Indicators

Economic Aspect of TBL

Economic development increase the GDP and spending power of people this results in consumption of resources leading to a negative environmental impact.

Designing for sustainability is dependent upon an understanding of the short- and long-term goals and values of individuals, institutions and governments.

It is about the big picture that allows economic activity to rise while:

reducing resource use and reducing environmental impact.

maintaining economic growth,

development,

improving productivity,

facilitates the economic trickle-down affect to local communities

Close cooperation is required between designer and manufacturer.

The importance of sustainability issues and strategies is critical to sustainable economic development.

Decoupling

Term: Decoupling refers to disconnecting two trends so that one no longer depends on the other. Through the act of decoupling (using resources more productively and redesigning production systems), it is technically possible to deliver the same or equivalent goods and services with lower environmental impact while maintaining social and equity benefits.

Decoupling is a strategy for sustainability

Consider the benefits and limitations of decoupling as an appropriate strategy for sustainability

Wikipedia on decoupling

Decoupling impacts and resources – from the UNEP

International and National Laws

The use of international and national laws to promote sustainable development

Nations need to adhere to the treaties/laws usually through enforceable domestic legislation.

International and national laws encourage companies to focus on something other than shareholder value and financial performance

Adopting a corporate strategy that has the support of shareholders/stakeholders can be difficult to achieve.

International and national laws encourage companies to focus on aspects other than shareholder value and financial performance,

These include transparency of corporate sustainability, transparent sustainability assurance and whether businesses, public services, national resources and the economy have the means to continue in the years ahead at a micro and macro level.

Kyoto Protocol on carbon emissions

Rio Earth Summit on sustainability

Sustainability Reporting

Term: A company report that focusses on four aspects of performance: Economic; Environmental; Social; and Governance.

A sustainability report is an organisation report that provides information on its performance in 4 areas:

Economic

Environmental

Social

Governance

The reliability and acceptance of sustainability reporting requires accurate data gathering to be maintained over a lengthy period of time.

Benefits of sustainability reporting for:

GovernmentsManufacturersConsumers

the information can be used to assess the impact on the economy, society and the environment

transparency, see what issues are being tackled

with the information can target areas of concern and help drive progress on sustainability

compliance with legislation

can drive innovation (product or systems) within an organisation

can use it as marketing

enhanced branding/reputation

potential cost savings

efficient governance and management

potential cheaper products or services

potential for more innovative products or services

builds trust in that organtisation

information can assure the consumer that it is globally and nationally employing sustainable practises and strategies

Coca Cola Sustainability Report

Crocs 2014 Sustainability Report

Product Stewardship

Product Stewardship at a company

Product Stewardship

Everyone involved in making, selling, buying or handling equipment (products) takes responsibility for minimizing environmental impact of the equipment at all stages in the life cycle.

Designers may need to respond to consumer pressure as more consumers become aware of resource issues and product labelling.

Some examples of product stewardship include:

Organic foods

Genetically modified food

Green cotton –

Article on Green Cotton in fashion

Forest stewardship –

Forest Stewardship Council

Bio-plastics

The following areas should be explored through case studies in terms of product stewardship:

NYC programme

Link to an AHA graphic (its big1)

International Mindedness

Changes in governments sometimes result in the reversal of sustainable development policies leading to different approaches to international agreements.

Theory of Knowledge

Design involves making value judgments in deciding between different ways of interacting with the environment. Is this the case in other areas of knowledge?

8.2 SUSTAINABLE CONSUMPTION

Designers develop products, services and systems that satisfy basic needs and improve quality of life. To meet sustainable consumption requirements, they must also minimize the use of natural resources, toxic materials and waste, and reduce emissions of pollutants at all stages of the life cycle.

It is not only the role of designers to create markets for sustainable products. Consumers need to change their habits and express a want and need for these products.

Sustainable Consumption

Term: The consumption of goods and services that have minimal environmental impact, promote social equity and economically viable, whilst meeting basic human needs worldwide.

Sustainable consumption is not about consuming less but consuming differently.

Designers need to recognize the importance of consumerism in developed countries and as an ambition in many developing countries.

Societies, particularly in developed countries, are [tend to be] a throwaway society.

Consumers need to be encouraged to repair and reuse products rather than throw them away.

Sustainable design and sustainable production contribute to sustainable consumption.

This can be achieved in a number of ways, for example, not buying more food than needed and reducing waste; changing attitudes to water and energy use, for example, turning taps off when brushing teeth, aerated water in showers, less water per flush of the toilet, grey water.

Consumer Attitudes

Consumer attitudes and behaviours towards sustainability can be classified into 4 groups.

Eco-warriors:

Term: Individuals or groups that actively demonstrate on environmental issues.

It is an individual who cares about our environment & the diversity of life forms so much that they want to take action.

An eco-warrior can be someone such as non-confrontational as a tree sitter or someone who engages in direct action, ranging anywhere from planting tree spikes into trees on public lands, to keep the lumber industry from cutting them down, to sit-ins which occupy a corporate office.

Eco-champions:

Term: Individuals or groups that champion environmental issues within organizations.

Champion environmental issues within organizations.

Attempt to introduce or create change in a product, process, or method that takes into account green or environmental issues

Is a person who fights or argues for a cause.

Eco-fans:

Term: Individuals or groups that enthusiastically adopt environmentally friendly practices as consumers.

It is usually someone who accepts all green design products on the current market or its related objectives.

An eco-fan will usually buy anything that is environmentally friendly and will never buy a harmful product.

Green Attitude to Buying Green – click on the image

Eco-phobes:

Term: Individuals or groups that actively resent talk of environmental protection.

Eco-phobes are people who are against helping the environment and purposely go against the ecological movements.

They believe that the environmental problems are irrelevant to their lives or are blown out of proportion.

Wikipedia reference to environmental denial

An example of an eco-phobe is a head of a country refusing to sign the Kyoto agreement which is based on controlling the c02 output in a country and limit it in order to decrease global warming.

Eco-Labelling and Energy Labelling Schemes

For the designer such labels can help guide their designing in order to meet country regulations or the manufacturers design specifications.

When designers design products they need to take into consideration the criteria that make up the different eco and energy labels for different labelling schemes.

For the consumer they can make the appropriate purchase if they are environmentally concerned. Different countries ahed different contexts.

International standardisation has resulted in many eco- and energy labelling schemes being similar thus easy for the consigner to understand.

Eco-labelling:

Term: The labelling of products to demonstrate that they are better for the environment than other products.

Provides reliable information about how the product impacts the environment, considering all stages of the product's life cycle: manufacture, distribution, use and disposal. An example of this is Swan eco-label.

Aids in the improvement of the workers have a role in the production's social and economic conditions, like the Fair Trade Labelling.

Informs customers about how the energy is produced, and whether it meets certain requirements, like those of The FANC energy eco-labelling scheme.

Allows consumers to make informed choices.

The European eco-label believes in sustainable development. They are based on the vision of greening non-food products all over Europe. The eco-label 'norms' are decided by the European Union Eco-labeling (EUEB). In Australia, Good Environmental Choice Australia (GECA)is committed to credible product information for sustainable development. It is the only environmental labeling program in Australia which indicates the environmental performance of a product during its complete life cycle. In the United States there is an eco label named Energy stars, which is a joint program of the U.S. Environmental Protection Agency and the U.S. Department of Energy that promotes energy efficient products and practices. The Nutriclean label means that products are tested

Energy-labelling:

Term: The labelling of products to show how energy efficient they are. The label displays information in four categories: the product's details; Energy classification that shows the product's electrical consumption; Measurements relating to consumption, efficiency and capacity etc.; Noise emitted from the product when in use.

The label provides/displays four pieces of information:

The product's details;

Energy classification that shows the product's electrical consumption;

Measurements relating to consumption, efficiency and capacity etc.;

Noise emitted from the product when in use.

It shows the user how much energy is required/used by a product, as well as how efficient it is (how much heat-loss for example)

By using such labels, consumers can make their choices in products, by taking into account how much energy (toll on the environment) is used by the product.

By comparing theses two labels. and with consumer help, more environmentally friendly products could be sold therefore making companies use greener design.

As with Eco-labelling this label is given by a third party company

Australian Energy Label

Market for Sustainable Products

Corporate strategies have an impact on the design brief or specifications, such as, market development, where we take an existing product and develop a new segment.

Creating a market for sustainable products:

pricing considerations: ensuring the products proved value-for-money to the customer.

such as an eBikes that use cheaper lead-acid batteries vs lithium ion batteries.

long term costs

For example incandescent bulbs are very cheap and long life bulbs tend to more expensive. The Incandescent bulbs need regular changing

stimulating demand for green products

consumers must be convinced that the green product is of similar or better quality

is competitively priced

promote their green products

production of green products

taking into consideration triple bottom line sustainability

JIT manufacturing

end-of-pipe or better still radical change to manufacturing

13 Sustainable products for 2013

Long life vs Incandescent bulbs power

Green Products

Pressure Groups

Collections of individuals who hold a similar viewpoint on a particular topic, for example the environment, who take action to promote positive change to meet their goals.

"Non-profit and usually voluntary organization whose members have a common cause for which they seek to influence political or corporate decision makers to achieve a declared objective. Whereas interest groups try to defend a cause (maintain the status quo), the pressure groups try to promote it (change the status quo)." (Business dictionary)

Pressure groups are not a market segment but they can influence the market and product cycle.

Some large organizations have evolved to inform consumers about environmental issues and ethical issues relating to the activities of certain multinational corporations.

These pressure groups are able to exert considerable influence to press for changes on these issues and to support or undermine development of specific technologies, for example, GM food production.

Consumer and environmental pressure groups can attract widespread support using the media (including social media).

Consumers have become increasingly aware of information provided by these organizations and, as markets have globalized, so has consumer power.

Advantages and disadvantages of consumer and environmental pressure groups for the user, manufacturer and designer

UserManufacturerDesigner

Advantages

new products (green or innovative)

in long run costs reduced

improve reputation of the company

Disadvantages

new products may cost more

products become obsolete

forced to develop new products

add costs due to changes in design or manufacturing

forced to change design ideas

constrained in creativity

Other Advantages

raise public awareness of environmental issues

can have large numbers of members that can exert pressure on political parties (small smaller in numbers)

can have expertise related tot he issues

Other Disadvantages

they may be biased towards their cause – not looking at both sides

sometimes not objective

make use extreme tactics or break the law

opinions on issues may not be representative of the wider community

Lifestyle and Ethical Consumerism

Ethical Consumerism: The practice of consciously purchasing products and services produced in a way that minimises social and environmental damage, while avoiding those that have a negative impact on society and the environment.

Lifestyle Consumerism: A social and economic order and ideology that encourages the acquisition of goods and services in ever greater amounts.

Consider strategies for managing western consumption while raising the standard of living of the developing world without increasing resource use and environmental impact.

Some companies incorporate ethics into their corporate strategy and designers need to work within such constraints.

They aim to curb and manage Western consumption while raising the standard of living of the developing world without increasing its resource use and environmental impact.

Implications of Take-Back Legislation for Designers, Manufacturers and Consumers

Take back legislation is the legislation that holds manufacturers responsible for the environmentally safe recycling or disposal of their end-of-life products. They are expected to provide a financial and/or physical plan to ensure that such products are collected and processed.

Apple, in 2016, introduced a take back program where you can get a discounted price on a new phone.

In Maine in the U.S.A., Car manufacturers have take-back legislation in the sense that they have to pay the collection and recycling of mercury switches from old cars.

In March 2003 the UK government issued a legislation requiring that all car manufacturer's and vehicle importers of new cars into the United Kingdom take back vehicles from their previous owner and guarantee that they are treated environmentally friendly.

In Sweden, Producers and importers must take back for free a piece of old equipment (all electrical household appliance) when the customer buys a new product.

In Japan, the end users are obliged to pay fees for collection, take-back and recycling at the time of disposal. The government sets the fees to cover industry's actual costs for take-back, transportation, and recycling. They are (in U.S. dollars): washing machine, $24; air conditioner, $35; refrigerator, $46; and television, $27.

LG Policy of recycling and take-back.

The implications for the design cycle and product cycle depend on the nature of appropriate legislation.

Impact for the designer ... when designing

Consider candle to the grave or cradle to cradle to cradle

Consider recyclability or re-use of materials

Consider design for disassembly

Work within the cost constraints if manufacturer – make the process efficient

Impact for the manufacturer ...

Added costs due to paying for it to be returned and recycled

Interested in design for disassembly and recyclability since they are most likely the ones pulling it apart and recycling or reusing

consider manufacturing techniques

consider material selection and reduction in products

collection systems need to be developed

manage the waste themselves or have a third party do it

Impact for the consumer ...

The extra costs may be passed onto he consumer

Must return the product

can rest assured that the environment is considered

International Mindedness

There are many different eco-labelling and energy-labelling schemes across the world that could be standardized

Theory of Knowledge

Eco-warriors sometimes break laws to express their views. Does the rightness or wrongness of an action depend on the situation?

8.3 SUSTAINABLE DESIGN

The first step to sustainable design is to consider a product, service or system in relation to eco-design and analyse its impact using life cycle analysis. The designer then develops these to minimize environmental impacts identified from this analysis. Considering sustainability from the beginning of the process is essential.

Datschefski's five principles of sustainable design equip the designer with a tool not only to design new products, but also to evaluate an existing product. This can lead to new design opportunities and increase the level at which a product aligns with these principles.

Green design versus sustainable design

Green design: is designing in a way that takes account of the environmental impact of the product throughout its life

Sustainable design is the philosophy of designing physical objects, the built environment, and services to comply with the principles of social, economic, and ecological sustainability. (Wikipedia)

Green DesignSustainable Design

Products that have little or no affect on the environment.Deals with TBL sustainability, economic, environmental & Social

Cradle to the grave approach Cradle to cradle approach

Shorter (than sustainable design) therefore easier and cheaper to address environmental concerns in products.Longer timescale which can affect the R & D stage (system wide research needed) of the design process increases costs therefore may not be feasible.

Incremental idea generating techniques are feasible as possibly only small changes need to be made.Idea generating techniques are more radical to re-think (over-haul/redesign) the nature of the product and ho it works

Datschefski's five principles of sustainable design

Students need to develop an understanding of Datschefski's five principles of sustainable design (The Total Beauty of Sustainable Products, 2001). The five principles are a holistic approach to sustainable design but only selected principles will be possible/applicable to some products.

Cyclic – The product could not only be made from recyclable materials but is also compostable, of organic materials or from minerals that are recycled in a continuous loop such as bio plastics.

Solar – The energy (both embedded and in use) the product requires comes form only renewable energy sources that is cyclic and safe.

Safe – By-products products of the that are emitted into the environment (air, land & water) and 'space' are non-hazardous, i.e. non polluting. The by-products are "food" for other systems. Hydrogen fuel celled cars' by-prodouct when in use is H2O.

Efficient – Requiring 90% less energy, materials and water than equivalent products in 1990.

Social – The products manufacture and usage should underpin basic human rights, safe work practises, fair trade principles and natural justice.

Bioplastic Life-cycle

Hydrogen Fuel Cell Car

International-mindedness

The application of Datschefski's social principle of sustainable design can have different effects across different countries.

Theory of knowledge

Datschefski developed his five principles of sustainable design to help designers structure their approach and thoughts. In what ways and areas would the absence of experts most severely limit our knowledge?

8.4 SUSTAINABLE INNOVATION

Sustainable innovation yields both bottom line and top line returns as developing products, services and systems that are environmentally friendly lowers costs through reducing the resources required. Designers should view compliance with government legislation as an opportunity for sustainable innovation.

As energy security becomes an ever more important issue for all countries, designers, engineers and inventors need to develop new ways of efficiently generating energy. As new energy production technologies become available, designers need to harness them to be used in new products to improve their energy efficiency.

Complexity and Timescale of Sustainable Innovation

Complexities:

Sustainable innovation relies on cooperation between different stakeholders such as government and manufacturing.

This is often difficult as both parties have differing views.

Sustainable innovation requires a radical change which is time-consuming and expensive so manufacturers are not so willing to consider sustainable innovation.

It is the broadest approach going beyond technical solutions. This approach is based on a socio-technical systems (interaction between people land technology) intervention rather than just considering product improvement.

Timescale:

The huge timescale means that sustainability is difficult to maintain as conditions/criteria can change significantly, for example, a lengthy period of economic downturn.

Sustainable innovation is a hugely complex concept that requires a long time for implementation, typically 20–40 years depending on the nature of the innovation.

Sustainable Strategies

Sustainable use of the planet will require multiple sustainability strategies, which will range from the entire system, the entire Earth, the local or regional.

Strategies starting at the highest system level are referred to as 'top-down', and strategies designed for components, local or regional, are referred to as 'bottom-up' Integrating top-down/bottom-up sustainability strategies: An ethical challenge (PDF Download Available). [accessed Nov 26, 2015].

Top-down strategies

Strategies implemented from the 'top' such as global or national government initiatives.

Management of resources, finances (controlling bank rates, etc) and so on.

It provides targets and measures for sustainability.

When considering sustainable innovation, designers are usually more comfortable with top-down strategies as it means investment and resources are more predictable and reliable.

Examples of top-down and bottom-up strategies and the advantages and disadvantages for consumers/users

Bottom-up strategies

Strategies implemented from the 'bottom' such as regional or local (city or town) level.

These include local initiatives like Planting Tree Campaigns

Designers involved with bottom-up strategies are usually enthusiasts for the project and willing to make a commitment even though it may not be cost-effective to do so.

Examples of top-down and bottom-up strategies and the advantages and disadvantages for consumers/users

Government intervention in innovation

There are various strategies that governments use to promote knowledge exchange and technology transfer, including:

regulation—setting and policing rules to avoid or limit environmental issues caused by undesirable technologies yet allow the manufacturer to still make profits

education—providing consumers with information and guidance in the choice of products and services that are more sustainable

such as eco and energy labels

taxes—to penalize environmentally damaging technologies and influence consumer choice of sustainable products and services

outside Beijing the government is forcing companies to comply or they are fined and ultimately closed down

subsidies—to stimulate and support sustainable innovations.

sustainable innovation can cast the company profits so governments offer financial help or tax breaks.

A potential problem for designers is the changing political scene and associated policies, for example, within the domain of renewable energy.

Macro energy sustainability

Macro energy sustainability concerns can be influenced through international treaties and current international energy policies, instruments for change and disincentives, and national systems changing policy when government leadership changes.

Kyoto Protocol on the reduction of green house gases.

In order for it to be successful all governments need to agree, for a while Australia and USA did not so many countries followed suit

Are there any other implications of how macro energy sustainability can be influenced?

Micro energy sustainability

Micro energy sustainability can be influenced by government, through their role in raising awareness and changing attitudes related to energy use and the promotion of individual and business action towards energy sustainability.

Local governments installing Combined Heat and Power (CHP)

Are there any other implications of how micro energy sustainability can be influenced?

Energy security

How energy security can be influenced by energy demand/supply trends and forecasting, demand response versus energy efficiency, and smart grids

Energy demand is rarely constant and this puts a responsibility on those that generate and manage the flow of energy to understand when peaks and troughs of energy use occur over the course of days, weeks and years.

For example, in many countries, energy demand increases substantially during breaks and following popular TV shows as large numbers of people put the kettle on to enjoy a hot beverage.

Also, there may be particular periods during the night where energy use is at a minimum. In these situations it is vital that the power-generating stations are informed when to start and stop energy generation.

The difficulty arises as massive amounts of electricity cannot easily be stored, excess energy generated at these times is wasted.

Demand/supply trends need to be predicted carefully to create a responsive and efficient energy supply.

International Mindedness

The internal policies of particular governments have international implications.

Theory of Knowledge

To what extent should environmental concerns limit our pursuit of knowledge?

CHAPTER NINE

Innovation & Markets

9.1 CORPORATE STRATEGIES

The success of a company relies heavily on the strategies it adopts. The evaluation of products, services and systems can inform the selection of the most appropriate strategies to follow that will enable a company to achieve its objectives.

The designer must consider the ethical implications of imitating the products of others and their implications on a cultural, economic, and intellectual property level.

The success of a company relies heavily on the corporate strategy it adopts. There are many different corporate strategies a company can consider.

Pioneering Strategy

Pioneering means being ahead of the competitors by introducing a new product or innovation into the market first.

Apple Newton and 1st Generation iPhone

Pioneering, a corporate strategy, is the process of introducing new areas of thought or development in the design process.

Motorola introduced the 1st mobile phone in 1973 and commercially in 1983.

It is the most risky (costly) strategy but one with the potential for the largest gains.

A pioneering company requires a strong research and development (R&D) capability, which is expensive.

A pioneering company needs to be financially secure and requires product champions to push new ideas.

Consider the Sony or Apple companies and their various pioneering developments.

Good market research can offset some risk, but is problematic for novel products.

To be successful while using this type of corporate strategy, the firm must learn more about the consumer market by extensive market research.

This is recommended because the pioneering strategy is very risky due to the fact the firm is introducing a totally new, unknown, and unexpected product or service to the market.

Although pioneering is risky and costly, the profits that can be earned from this strategy balances with the risks

The risk of failure is considerably high because this product or service has never entered the market, thus making it is impossible to determine that the product will be a success or failure since the product/service's lack of experience in the market.

Apple: In an interview, the CEO was asked if he was concerned that so many companies produced very similar products after Apple's releases. His reply was, no, as it shows that we are pioneering and ahead of the rest.

Imitative Strategy

The imitative strategy aims to develop a product similar to the "pioneered" product (an existing new product) as quickly as possible. It takes advantage of R&D invested by others, and is less risky, but is based on a strong development capability.

When the apple iPhone came out within months many of the other smartphone companies adopted similar touch screen technology, apps, and aesthetic principles.

1st Generation iPhone released in 2007

Samsung 1st Generation Smartphone released in 2008

The Success of Pioneering and Innovative Strategies

Consider the success of each between the two

The Success of Pioneering and Innovative Strategies

Examples of companies and products that have used the above strategies – Apple vs Samsung

The Apple iPod is an example of a product developed using a pioneering strategy. At the time, there were no similar products on the market. As Apple has continued to develop products such as the iPhone and iPad, many electronics companies have mimicked the aesthetic style and functionality of their products.

Hybrid Strategy

There are many benefits for a company using a hybrid strategy. Companies that use a mixture of pioneering, imitative strategies or any of the below ones listed, in order to:

maximize profit and sales

provides for a quick turn around

reduces R&D spending

reduces the risk of employing only a pioneering strategy.

Activity 9.1a: Describe a product that has been produced that was/is similar to an existing product (other than an Apple product) that was pioneering. Also, consider the relative success of the pioneering strategy.

Activity 9.1b: Describe a product that has been produced that was/is similar to an existing product (other than a Samsung product) that was imitative. Also, consider the relative success of a imitative strategy.

Activity9.1c: Describe a product that has been produced that are a result of a hybrid approach. Also, consider the relative success of a hybrid approach.

Market and Product Growth Strategies

Knowledgegrab on Ansoff Matrix for product and market growth strategies.

Market Penetration

Increasing sales to existing customers or finding new customers for an existing product.

For example, if there are 300 million people in a country and 65 million of those people have cell phones then the market penetration of cell phones would be approximately 22%. This would mean in theory there are still 235 million more potential customers for cell phones, which may be a good sign of growth for cell phone makers. In general, the older the offering or industry, the greater the market penetration. Web reference

Describe a strategy that a company would use to enhance market penetration.

A strategy a company may consider to enhance market penetration is product promotion.

Product promotion engages in propagating information about a product, product line, brand, or company.

More examples on market penetration.

Market Development

The video is good in illustrating market penetration although it does focus on the negative affects.

Finding new applications for existing products, thereby opening up new markets

Market development targets customers in a market segment who are not buying the companies products, for example Apple iPhone targeting Blackberry customers in the smartphone market segment.

Market development targets customers in other market segments such as Apple iPod customers being targeted by the iPhone.

Describe how a company would undertake market development.

The identification of new markets for products,

For example, nylon was originally developed for parachutes and now have varied uses including clothing, sports etc.

Activity9.1d: Locate a product that was or still is used in one market and that was later used in a different market or product.

Product Development

The creation of new, modified or updated products aimed mainly at a company's existing customers.

Describe one example of how a company undertakes product development.

Consider adding variations to a product to develop a range of products building on an established brand,

For example, ice cream, snack food products, chocolate products (Kit Kat, Mars bars).

Variety of flavours from Coca-cola products

Product development, can be approached through many ways:

By enhancing the released product, adding new features i.e a camera on a phone, or video playback on an I-pod.

By increasing the products range, giving different designs and/or adding more options to certain ones.

The company may release many different types, of a certain general product, even if they are very different i.e different soda flavours under the same company name.

Activity9.1e: Describe a product that has been modified or updated products aimed mainly at a company's existing customers.

Product Diversification

Increasing sales from new products [and]/or [new] markets

Involves a company both in the development of new products and in selling those products to new companies.

High risk strategy.

Describe one example of diversification.

a company manufacturing three-pin electrical plugs may consider producing them in a range of colours or from materials of different textures and/or material properties. (need to find a different example)

Activity9.1f: Locate an example of a product that was a result of diversification.

Ansoff Matrix

Ansoff Matrix of 4 growth strategiesCoca-Cola strategies example from marketingagenda

Corporate Social Responsibility

Corporate social responsibility is a form of self-regulation for a company and centres around the development of goals related to three areas:

economic

social

environmental

Companies that consider corporate social responsibility as a goal need to assess the impact of their operations in relation to these three areas in order to maximize the benefits and minimize the disadvantages.

Students need to consider the ways in which a company might achieve this and the evidence of effective corporate social responsibility for a major multinational corporation.

How corporate social responsibility may be a particular goal of a company whereby the aim is to manage the economic, social and environmental impacts of their operation to maximize the benefits and minimize the disadvantages

Examples of evidence of effective corporate social responsibility for a major multinational company

10 examples of CSR

2018 Most Ethical Companies

International Mindedness

Adoption of corporate social responsibility by multinational companies can be used as a distraction from their core business practices.

Theory of Knowledge

Is strategic planning more influenced by reason, intuition or imagination? Or by a combination of all of the ways of knowing?

9.2 MARKET SECTORS AND SEGMENTS

Designers must consider the market when targeting their product, service or system. The smaller the sector, the more the target audience will have in common. Companies may decide to compete in the whole market or only in segments that are attractive and/or familiar. A designer's understanding of the identified market is essential.

By identifying the market sectors and segments a product will be designed for, a designer can gain data directly from the perspective of the potential consumer.

Market Sector

Market Sector: A broad way of categorizing the kinds of market the company is aiming for.

Categories of market sectors

Designers need to clearly be able to identify the needs of the target market and target audience. These can be classified into two categories:

Geographical sectors, which focus on the values, culture and characteristics of purchasers in that region along with purchasing power

Consumer needs vary between climatic regions where block heaters are used in Canada which would be of little use in Egypt

Client-based sectors, which may focus on consumers, industrial, public sector and commercial.

Watchmakers target income groups such as Tissot vs Swatch.

List of Sectors from yahoo. Click on the sector and you will see smaller sections.

Block heaters for cars

Tissot vs Swatch Watch – Client based sector

The influence of market sectors

if there is a technological advance then the products or services in that sector will change.

This change will influence the target markets.

Such as the size of microchips allowing for powerful portable devices leading to iPads and smartphones.

Products in Sectors

Products designed to be sold in one sector for example laptops would fall under the technology sector.

Products designed to be sold to more than one sector for example an iPhone – technology and telecommunication sectors.

How multinational companies take into account market sectors in the design and manufacture of their products.

The difference between a market sector and market segment

Market sector is a broad way of categorising the kinds of market the company is aiming for. The sectors have similar characteristics such a technology, utilities, telecommunications etc

Market sector explained on investopedia

Market segment is dividing up the markets into smaller segments targeting customers that share characteristics.

They interact with one another by nature of their characteristics. Technology sector would govern who the segments are targeting, i.e. early adopters, gamers, etc. This in turn could influence the direction of the companies in the sector head.

Classifications of consumer market segments

Maket segmentation: Markets divided in to smaller segments where purchasers have similar characteristics and/or tastes.

Market segmentation described by the Open University. Explains well why and how businesses can target segments.

A slideshare an intern on market segmentation.

The fact that the consumer market is divided in segments allows companies and organisations to develop promotional campaigns targeting specific segments.

For example business people for business class on airlines or executive automobiles.

This means the company can develop products that better suit the consumer of segment.

Types of Market Segments

income (high, middle and low levels of finance) – Daewoo and Corolla vehicles for price sensitive customers whereas Mercedes and BMW aim their cars at the more affluent.

profession (types of jobs one has which can influence social groups or personal interests) – marketing e-book for executives,

age (babies, toddlers, tweens, teenagers, young adults, middle aged to the elderly) – such as diapers/nappies for babies, toys for children, clothes for teenagers

family – (single no kids, single kids, married two kids, empty nesters etc) – a family with kids would purchase furniture that is more family orientated as opposed to a single living alone (trendy furniture).

values (the ethical, worthiness or importance of something that is held by an individual or group, opinions) – environmentally friendly products vs a throw away society.

behaviour (shopping mannerisms, loyalty, occasion buying, such as impulsive, online vs brick 'n mortar, or the researcher) – buying turkeys at christmas and thanksgiving (occasion buying), Apple customers (loyalty),

An idea list for segments – by no means an exhaustive list

Demographic Segmentation

How the needs of the market segments listed above impact on the design of products and scale of production.

In China there is a need of low cost street commuter bicycles (no gears, basket, simple brakes) to cater for a market segment of low income earners which is a large target market. The scale of production would be that of volume.

Mont Blanc pens target a market segment of middle to high income earners and possibly business men and women. These would be batch produced. The cheapest at an UK online pen store in April 2015 was £170. Whereas a a box of 60 Bic pens in the USA costs $15. These would be volume produced.

The development of a product family

Product family: A group of products having common classification criteria. Members normally have many common parts, assemblies and/or aesthetic elements.

Companies and designers will develop a successful product or product range into product families. This further develops a successful market segment that is already familiar with the original product. For example, iPod then IPhone,, then iPad.

Designers often develop product families to extend a successful product range and to develop products for market segments that are already familiar with the original product.

Apple Product Family

Windows Product Family

International-mindedness:

Two broad categories of market sectors are geographical- and client-based, with specific segments varying greatly.

Theory of knowledge:

Gaining information on market sectors often employs many of the methods of gaining knowledge most closely associated with the human sciences. What are these methods of gaining knowledge, and how do they compare to the methods used in the natural sciences?

Something Extra

Mashable Infographic

Designers must consider the market when targeting their product, service or system. The smaller the sector, the more the target audience will have in common. Companies may decide to compete in the whole market or only in segments that are attractive and/or familiar. A designer's understanding of the identified market is essential.

By identifying the market sectors and segments a product will be designed for, a designer can gain data directly from the perspective of the potential consumer.

Market Sector

Market Sector: A broad way of categorizing the kinds of market the company is aiming for.

Categories of market sectors

Designers need to clearly be able to identify the needs of the target market and target audience. These can be classified into two categories:

Geographical sectors, which focus on the values, culture and characteristics of purchasers in that region along with purchasing power

Consumer needs vary between climatic regions where block heaters are used in Canada which would be of little use in Egypt

Client-based sectors, which may focus on consumers, industrial, public sector and commercial.

Watchmakers target income groups such as Tissot vs Swatch.

List of Sectors from yahoo. Click on the sector and you will see smaller sections.

Block heaters for cars

Tissot vs Swatch Watch – Client based sector

The influence of market sectors

if there is a technological advance then the products or services in that sector will change.

This change will influence the target markets.

Such as the size of microchips allowing for powerful portable devices leading to iPads and smartphones.

Products in Sectors

Products designed to be sold in one sector for example laptops would fall under the technology sector.

Products designed to be sold to more than one sector for example an iPhone – technology and telecommunication sectors.

How multinational companies take into account market sectors in the design and manufacture of their products.

The difference between a market sector and market segment

Market sector is a broad way of categorising the kinds of market the company is aiming for. The sectors have similar characteristics such a technology, utilities, telecommunications etc

Market sector explained on investopedia

Market segment is dividing up the markets into smaller segments targeting customers that share characteristics.

They interact with one another by nature of their characteristics. Technology sector would govern who the segments are targeting, i.e. early adopters, gamers, etc. This in turn could influence the direction of the companies in the sector head.

Classifications of consumer market segments

Maket segmentation: Markets divided in to smaller segments where purchasers have similar characteristics and/or tastes.

Market segmentation described by the Open University. Explains well why and how businesses can target segments.

A slideshare an intern on market segmentation.

The fact that the consumer market is divided in segments allows companies and organisations to develop promotional campaigns targeting specific segments.

For example business people for business class on airlines or executive automobiles.

This means the company can develop products that better suit the consumer of segment.

Types of Market Segments

income (high, middle and low levels of finance) – Daewoo and Corolla vehicles for price sensitive customers whereas Mercedes and BMW aim their cars at the more affluent.

profession (types of jobs one has which can influence social groups or personal interests) – marketing e-book for executives,

age (babies, toddlers, tweens, teenagers, young adults, middle aged to the elderly) – such as diapers/nappies for babies, toys for children, clothes for teenagers

family – (single no kids, single kids, married two kids, empty nesters etc) – a family with kids would purchase furniture that is more family orientated as opposed to a single living alone (trendy furniture).

values (the ethical, worthiness or importance of something that is held by an individual or group, opinions) – environmentally friendly products vs a throw away society.

behaviour (shopping mannerisms, loyalty, occasion buying, such as impulsive, online vs brick 'n mortar, or the researcher) – buying turkeys at christmas and thanksgiving (occasion buying), Apple customers (loyalty),

An idea list for segments – by no means an exhaustive list

Demographic Segmentation

How the needs of the market segments listed above impact on the design of products and scale of production.

In China there is a need of low cost street commuter bicycles (no gears, basket, simple brakes) to cater for a market segment of low income earners which is a large target market. The scale of production would be that of volume.

Mont Blanc pens target a market segment of middle to high income earners and possibly business men and women. These would be batch produced. The cheapest at an UK online pen store in April 2015 was £170. Whereas a a box of 60 Bic pens in the USA costs $15. These would be volume produced.

The development of a product family

Product family: A group of products having common classification criteria. Members normally have many common parts, assemblies and/or aesthetic elements.

Companies and designers will develop a successful product or product range into product families. This further develops a successful market segment that is already familiar with the original product. For example, iPod then IPhone,, then iPad.

Designers often develop product families to extend a successful product range and to develop products for market segments that are already familiar with the original product.

Apple Product Family

Windows Product Family

International-mindedness:

Two broad categories of market sectors are geographical- and client-based, with specific segments varying greatly.

Theory of knowledge:

Gaining information on market sectors often employs many of the methods of gaining knowledge most closely associated with the human sciences. What are these methods of gaining knowledge, and how do they compare to the methods used in the natural sciences?

9.3 MARKETING MIX

Empathy for, and understanding of the target audience is developed through thorough analysis of the market chosen. This informs several factors: the standards that end users demand; how and where to distribute and sell the product; how much they are willing to pay for a certain product and its quality; and how to communicate the launch of a product. Correct analysis of these factors could determine the success or failure of a product, despite its quality.

Marketing is often a new area for designers to consider. Exploring unfamiliar aspects of innovation improves their understanding of the market needs of the products they are designing.

Marketing mix

The "marketing mix" involves 4 variables or 4 P's which are product, place, price and promotion.

A company will through market research using these variables so the designer has an accurate brief of the requirements of the market. Helps to develop a marketing strategy.

Mindtools has a great set of questions to ask/research for Criterion For your project

The 4Ps:

Product: standardization of products

Place: implications of internet selling for a company in relation to its supply chain and distribution network.

Price: cost-plus, demand pricing, competitor-based pricing, product line pricing, psychological pricing.

Promotion: advertising, publicity, personal selling.

Marketing Agenda Website has an Amazon example and explanation.

Product

Product Standardisation "The process of setting generally uniform characteristics for a particular good or service. Product standardization among the goods provided by different businesses operating in technology-based industries can be useful for consumers since it permits competition among the various suppliers." – from the Business Dictionary

The standardization of products is perform in three ways ...

1. Government standards for a particular market segment:

Is where a governments sets standards for products. For example in Europe that need to set a Health and Safety standard for a product as not to harm the user. It is the CE mark on most electrical devices.

The CE mark can be used in other countries such as China. Take a look at your mobile phone. So to the website for more information.

EU Standard

2. Component standardization:

Is where a part standardised,

e.g. USB ports or plugs, so they can be used in different or similar products, such as memory sticks or computers.

USB Standards

3. Industry-wide standards:

For a period architects and engineers would ask steel companies for all sorts of sectional beams for buildings.

This became inefficient and expensive.

So the steel industry in agreement with the architects and engineers developed a limited range of sectional beams.

Sectional Beams for buildings

Consider examples of trigger products and incremental products.

Place

The location of the product where it will be sold that is convenient for the customer. This could be:

Bricks and Mortar

a physical location such as a store

Boutique, chain, super or hyper makes, etcAdvantages:

you can try/touch/see it in real life.

Find similar products nearby

Disadvantages:

commute to store (find parking),

higher price (store cover costs of rent, distribution, etc)

time for travel and shopping around

Online (internet)

such as Taobao or Amazon

Companies need to ensure/plan for a supply chain and distribution network. If the supply chain breaks time it will delay the delivery the product to the customer.

News Article from the IndependentAdvantages:

Convenience: can shop from anywhere

Possibly lower prices

Disadvantages:

Shipping time and costs

Returns if the item is not what you expected

Cost incurred for returns

Hybrid Model

There is a shop front perhaps in a mall but they also have an online presence as well.

Direct from the manufacturer

Price

An extremely important aspect of marketing a product is setting the correct price that will attract consumers to make a purchase while generating profit. Without getting the balance right, a company can quickly find that they are losing money through lack of sales or through lack of profit generation. The following strategies for setting price can be used:

Calculate costs

Cost-plus pricing

This is where a company will add a percentage to the total costs for a product as a profit margin.

Total costs include: production/manufacture, design, distribution etc.

Example: If the total cost of the product is $500 and the company wants a 10% profit then the final cost for the consumer would be $550.

Demand pricing

Is where a a company sets the price according to the demand for the product

Initially the price my be high to maximise profits. If demand wanes then the price will be lower to diffuse into the wider market.

Examples include smartphones like the IPhone or gaming consoles. They start of high because of the high desirability of the product but as the time passes desirability wanes or new technology (to introduced in new similar products) then price is lowered.

Competitor-based pricing

Is where a company prices its product based on or in comparison to the price of similar (competitor) products.

It may be price below, same as or higher that similar products.

Costs to produce similar products will be about the same except there may be other features included, thus affecting the price or increasing desirability.

Examples include smartphones

Product line pricing

It is where a company sets the different prices for different products within a product line (a group of related products).

Example: a base price for a basic model, the next product up might have more features or be a better quality – it would be a higher price, and so on throughout the line. Computers, where different models may cater for different consumers.

Psychological pricing.

Is where a company sets a price for a product so the consumer feels they are paying less. Example: A pair of shoes are priced at $45.99 as opposed to $46

Promotion

When selling a product, promotion is another key aspect. Depending on the nature of a product, its position within the product life cycle among other reasons, the forms of promotion can be different.

These include:

advertising – an audio or visual form of marketing communication

publicity – giving out information about the product

personal selling – Door-to-door salesman, market stalls,

Examples of promotion campaigns for different products

Advertisement

International-mindedness:

When developing marketing campaigns, companies take account of different cultures and sectors in the target market.

Theory of knowledge:

Some advertisers emphasize the "science" behind their products. Does this suggest that some people may see scientific knowledge as being more reliable than knowledge in other areas of knowledge?

9.4 MARKET RESEARCH

Market research often identifies how to improve the product, service or system and increase its chance of success within a particular sector or segment. The price a user is prepared to pay is usually determined through market research. This in turn sets an upper limit of cost to the design and production of a potential product, service or system. Market research has a crucial role in determining the constraints a designer has to work within.

Often designers will work on projects that have new and radically unfamiliar contexts. This will deepen their understanding of market research, equipping them with a range of tools and skills that they can employ in many areas of life and empowering them as lifelong learners.

Types of Data

Primary vs Secondary

Qualitative vs Quantitative

Purpose of market research

There are many purposes of market research.

Gathering information in order to be able to generate new ideas for a product

Evaluating the market potential of products at various stages of development

Developing ideas into products to suit market requirements

Identifying suitable promotional strategies

Gathering information relating to demographics

Gathering information relating to family roles

Collecting data relating to economic trends

Taking into account technological trends and scientific advances

Gathering information about consumers

Considering consumers' reactions to technology and green design and the subsequent impact on design development and market segmentation

Relate these purposes to your own project work.

Consumers' reaction

To technology

Technophile: Someone who immediately welcomes a technological change – early adopters.

Technocautious: Someone who needs some convincing before embracing technological change – majority to late majority

Technophobe: Someone who resists all technological change – laggards.

Green design:

Eco-warriors actively demonstrate on environmental issues

Eco-champions champion environmental issues within organizations

Eco-fans enthusiastically adopt environmentally friendly practices as consumers.

Eco-phobes actively resent talk of environmental protection

These attitudes have a subsequent impact on design development and market segmentation. This will direct the companies products to certain target markets.

Article on Cultivating the Green Consumer that consumer demand for green products.

Market research strategies

Understanding that market research is a key element of the design project, students need to select from a range of strategies that will help them find out what the client wants and needs. It is important to note that often, what the client thinks they want and what they need can be very different things. There are many strategies for the student to identify the need, which include:

Literature search:

The use of consumer reports and newspaper items to follow historical development. Useful sources of information could include CD-ROMs, such as encyclopaedias and newspapers, or more specific disks, subject-specific magazines and manufacturers' information.

many sources of information are available

there may be an abundance of data, which can be too time-consuming.

Data can be both qualitative or quantitative

Expert appraisal:

The reliance on the knowledge and skills of an expert in the operation of the product. For example, expert knowledge and advice are gained (compared to a user trial), but the expert may be biased.

Expert knowledge can help decide design direction.

It may also be difficult to locate an expert.

Data is usually qualitative.

User trial:

The observation of people using a product and collection of comments from people who have used a product.

The "user" is a non-specialist, which makes trials easier and cost-effective.

However, users may carry out tasks in different ways from those expected and be inexperienced.

Data is usually qualitative.

User research:

Obtaining users' responses through questionnaires/surveys and interviews.

It is cheap and quick to conduct

The data collect if qualitative or statistics can be produced (quantitative)

Perceptual mapping:

Quickly compare a product to others in the market due to it being a graphical representation.

It is simple and easy to construct.

It is qualitative as it examines consumer perceptions.

Could be biased.

Environmental scanning:

Slideshare on Environmental scanning

Environmental analysis is careful study of various factors influencing the business. It is the process by which organization monitor their relevant environment to identify opportunities and threats affecting their business.

Disadvantages include lack of detailed information or specifics of what constitutes these opportunities or threats it may need much more research or specific data to identify usable information. – not yet ready needs fixing.

Students need to draw from the above list when identifying a design opportunity and, prior to this, must have developed an understanding of these strategies. To this end, they should consider the advantages and disadvantages of the research strategies listed above in relation to the nature, reliability and cost of the research and importance to the design development process.

International Mindedness

Determining the purpose of market research allows designers to clearly identify who needs to be included and their differing requirements.

Theory of Knowledge

What are the assumptions that underlie methods used to gain knowledge in this area?

9.5 BRANDING

In order to diffuse products into the marketplace, the identity of a company is typically embodied in a brand. The brand is communicated to the consumer through a value proposition. Designers help to communicate this by: building a strong user experience around the brand identity; determining content design; establishing the tone of message through advertisements; promotion.

A brand encapsulates the identity of a company and its products. The brand designer needs to ensure that the message of a company is communicated clearly and creatively to allow them to stand out from the competition.

Brand: A product from a known source (organization). The name of the organization can also serve as a brand.

The role of the designer varies when taking into account brand image/identity

depending on the position of the new design within the innovation cycle.

there are many different brands that are appealing to different market segments

thus will use different methods to promote loyalty.

Brand loyalty

Brand Loyalty: Where a person has a favourite supplier and prefers to buy products from them rather than from other suppliers.

Brand Loyalty

Definition from Investopedia:

Brand loyalty is a result of consumer behavior and is affected by a person's preferences.

Loyal customers will consistently purchase products from their preferred brands, regardless of convenience or price.

This is based on perception where the consumer will continue to repurchase the product as it is perceived to be superior to its competitors.

Examples of brand loyalty

Coke vs Pepsi

Apple Mac vs Windows PCs

MacDonalds vs Burger King

iPhone vs Android/Samsung

Interestingly, brand loyalty is not specific to a company but rather to it's product, for example, a consumer may find Nike football (soccer) boots the best but Adidas sports shoes as preferred cross trainers.

Developing brand loyalty: Coca- cola, "Happiness in a bottle" and "Share a Coke", is one of the globally recognised brands around.

Went from selling 9 bottles to billions in a year.

Here are an article on the 7 strategies that made it such a recognisable brand and another from InterBrand

A vintage American ad

Take the Poll!

How brands appeal to different market segments

Suitable strategies for market research are important in gaining appropriate information for redesigning products.

When designing a brand it is important to identify the needs and wants of the market segment the product is aiming towards.

A product may require a different brand identity depending on the market segment they are targeting.

On occasion, products will be rebranded for different segments based on:

geographic location – international or local – urban or rural

age – teens, tweens, elderly, etc

gendcr

culture – National or sub culture

McDonalds Market segmentation and Marketing Mix

Mcdonalds has meals based on the future of the market.

What are some examples?

There are many brands that appeal to different market segments.

Lets look at the family car market segment.

Which brand is targeting which market segment

BMW

VW Touran

Volvo

Honda CRV

Activity:

Discuss the following points

Which one would you choose?

What kind of market segment are the brands targeting?

Why is one brand targeting that particular market?

Which one is the best?

Is there another market segment you can think of?

Contribution of packaging to brand identity.

Packaging contributes to brand identity. It helps companies to communicate their brand so that is highly recognisable.

Being highly recognisable allows for products to be easily seen and the point if sale. such as supermarkets which are inundated with soda options like Coca-Cola and Pepsi.

Good and unique packaging design will help promote this.

Companies will employ teams that design the packaging usually in conjunction with the branding department.

Sometimes the packaging may be outsourced to specialist packaging designers.

Where is Uncle Toby's? Here is is so it is instantly recognised amongst other similar products.

Apple Packaging that is quality, solid and aesthetically pleasing. Promotes brand name, identity and loyalty.

Trademark and Registered design

Starbucks Brand Infringement

A brand is very important to business as it forms a product's identity. Starbucks Brand Infringement

They become extremely valuable such as 61% of Cola Colas' worth is its brand (mentioned in the earlier youtube video).

A brand is important to a product. and can promote sales.

If a customer is loyal to a brand then they are likely to continue to purchase other products from that Brand. Apple, is a good example where many Mac laptop owners are likely to have bought an iPhone or iPad.

As a result a brand image (e.g. the 'Nike Swoosh') becomes a commodity in itself which then becomes intellectual property, i.e. it needs protecting.

Trademark and registered design (see explanation below) infringements are wide spread with often the smallest or subtle changes to the trademark or restored design.

Infringements of trademarks and registered designs is quite commonplace for a wide range of products and some designers use their creativity to attempt to subtly disguise the infringement.

Coca Cola Bottle

Registered Design:

An intellectual property mark that protects a product's appearance.

This refers to the features of the product's shape, configuration, pattern or ornamentation which is new and distinctive.

Coca Cola is an example where the Font and shape of the bottle are protected.

Trademark

"A trademark is a word, symbol, or phrase, used to identify aparticular manufacturer or seller's products and distinguish them from the products of another. 15 U.S.C. � 1127. For example, the trademark "Nike," along with the Nike "swoosh," identify the shoes made by Nike and distinguish them from shoes made by other companies (e.g. Reebok or Adidas)". From Harvard University Law

Trademarks and Registered Design are applied in terms of branding. Trademarks and Registered Designs not only help to protect a products image but but can be used product diversification. A Nike has a range of sports apparel (not just shoes) so a protected trademark can be used on shirts, pants, socks etc. You will see these symbols attached to a product branding features. Have a close look at coca cola or nike.

Publicity on brand image

There are many implications for a company of positive and negative publicity on brand image.

Article on Brand Image

A big challenge for designers is to maintain or improve the brand image while creating an innovative new product—this is sometimes achieved through the corporate strategy of diversification.

In other words, to mitigate negative publicity on brand in one market segment which is enjoying positive publicity in another market segment.

Positive publicity obviously doesn't hurt. Apple has had its fair share of publicity both negative and positive. The Positive publicity of it being an innovator, iWatch amongst other products, (Boston Globe article) allows it home forgiveness when negative publicity hits such as the iPhone 6 bending issues, dubbed BendGate (TechTimes article).

Negative publicity can diminish positive consumer perceptions of a brand. McDonalds brand image suffered for a while due environmental impact and healthy food issues. It has made big efforts to turn this around and maintain brand loyalty, this Prezi on McDonalds Brand will illustrate this. Other companies include Exxon and BP oil spills, Ford motors (exploding tyres), Toyota and more.

Activity:

Find a company that has had negative or positive publicity on its brand.

Write a sentence outlining how it affected the brand

Post it on the Padlet

Effects of product branding

Successful branding will promote how customers feel about a product or brand

Based on previous positive experience customers will buy well-known brands

Branding can promote the company

Branding and generate sales – perhaps of other products or product family

Examples of positive and negative effects of product branding on different market segments. – Health?? Spending money?? could these be effects?

Evaluating Global impact of branding

Look at examples of products affected by branding on a global scale.

Coca-Cola and Nike have become world leaders and have achieved market dominance and global recognition through branding

Brands need to be more socially and culturally aware now that they have gone global.

Swimwear companies marketing and selling their products in Italy may not be appropriate for Middle Eastern countries.

Language differences cause many problems for marketers in designing advertising campaigns and product labels.

Colors can have different meanings in different cultures which needs to considered to make sure the local consumers are not offended or pushed away from the product.

Cultures have a unique set of customs and taboos.

Boundless of global branding and marketing – good coverage of topics.

Forbes List of most recognisable and wealthy global brands

Market research on a global scale may be a time-consuming and expensive exercise, which is a major problem for innovative new companies, especially those reliant upon the internet for selling their product(s).

International Mindedness

A globally recognized and appealing brand allows organizations and companies to engage with global markets. This raises ethical issues with some products.

CHAPTER TEN

Commercial Production

10.1 JIT & JIC

While inventory creates a safety net for companies, maintenance and potential waste of resources can have significant implications for companies and the environment. Manufacturers must evaluate and analyse each market and determine whether a JIT or JIC strategy is the best to follow.

JIT and JIC are two production strategies used by manufacturers that have both advantages and disadvantages to them. A manufacturing company will choose one of these strategies to follow for many reasons that include the products they are producing, the nature of the market and the nature of the economy.

JIT vs JIC

Just in Time (JIT)

A situation where a company does not allocate space to the storage of components or completed items,

Instead orders or manufactures them when required.

Large storage areas are not needed

Items that are not ordered by customers are not made.

More information from this website.

Advantages

Storage – no space required thus reducing costs

Efficiency – Highly flexible, easy set-up for short runs (because of cell production)

Stock control – none required also no left over stock one the product becomes obsolete.

Waste – elimination of waste due to overproduction, left over stock, idle time, product defects and material processing.

Traditions – Factory organised in cells/modules instead of departments based on function

Disadvantages

Reliability – Part will need to be made, things could go wrong, delay in manufacture and transport to consumer

Capital investment – high but machinery could be used for a variety of products

Distribution – small delay as consumer waits for the manufacture and distribution.

JIT

A comparison

Just in Case (JIC)

A company produces a small stock of components or products and stores them as inventory.

This is Just-InCase a rush order comes they have ready supply.

Some products included may be products or components that take a long time to produce therefore reducing customer wait time.

Advantages

Distribution – no delay as as parts are available.

Reliability – Part is ready to be sent and probably has passed quality control.

Market demand – manufacturer is able to keep up with a change in market demand

Disadvantages

Efficiency – Not as effeiecwet as it is organised in departments often offsite.

Capital investment – high but machinery could be used for a variety of products

Storage – space required thus increasing costs

Waste -some waste due to overproduction, left over stock, product defects and material processing.

Traditions – Factory organised in departments based on function usually offsite bringing about added costs and transportation time

Stock control – required also, may left over stock one the product becomes obsolete or market direction changes.

International Mindedness

Effective business processes and practices developed in some countries have been exported successfully.

Theory of Knowledge

Manufacturers decide whether to pursue JIT or JIC as a production strategy depending on their perception of where the market is going. To what extent do different areas of knowledge incorporate doubt as a part of their methods?

10.2 LEAN PRODUCTION

Lean production considers product and process design as an ongoing activity and not a one-off task, and should be viewed as a long-term strategy.

The role of the workforce in lean production is paramount, relying on their wisdom and experience to improve the process, reducing waste, cost and production time. Recognizing this results in motivated workforces whose interests are in the success of the product.

Characteristics of lean production

Lean production considers product and process design as an ongoing activity and not a one-off task. It should be viewed as a long-term strategy that focuses on continual feedback and incremental improvement.

The characteristics of lean production include:

JIT supplies/system

a highly trained, multi-skilled workforce

quality control and continuous improvement

zero defects

zero inventory

Lean Production

Ten Principles of lean production

There are several key principles of lean production. If any of these principles are not met this could result in failure or a lack of commitment. Without commitment the process becomes ineffective.

Elimination of waste from various areas (JIT) and do it well from the beginning.

Minimizing inventory

Maximizing production flow and designing for rapid production changeover

Kaizan – Continuous Improvement from everyone – from management to workers. Without continuous improvement your progress will cease.

Respect for workers or empowering workers (Humans, most reliable and valuable resource to any company)

Pulling production from customer demand or meeting customer requirements

Designing for rapid changeover

Creating a reliable partnership with suppliers

Meeting customer requirements

Doing it right the first time

Advantages and disadvantages to lean production

Advantages

Increase consumer satisfaction due to cost reduction

Productivity has increased because of focus improvements and reduction in waste

Quality of product improvement and continuos improvement

Waste reduction

Reduced impact on the environment

Adapt to market pull

Increase in profits

Improved work conditions for employees

Competitive advantage

Disadvantages

Change in worker and management attitude can be difficult to manage or to gain complete buy in

Delivery times – since no inventory is held in storage and breakdown in the system will cause delays

Supply problems

High initial capital costs

Value Stream Mapping & Workflow Analysis

Value stream mapping is a lean production management tool used to analyse current and future processes for the production of a product through to delivery to the consumer.

helps to identify Value and Waste in production

Workflow analysis is the review of processes in a workflow,

for example, a production line,

in order to identify potential improvements.

Value stream mapping and workflow analysis contribute to the design of an effective lean production method through:

Value stream mapping provides the big picture of the manufacturing process

Where as workflow analysis is concerned with the production lines

Value Stream Map

This image shows a workflow analysis by using a flow chart through certain questions and criterions.

Product family

A group of products having common classification criteria.

Members of a product family have many common parts and assemblies and production processes.

Investopedia on Product Family

Advantages include:

Cost-effective due to – reduced manufacturing costs, similar manufacturing techniques, similar supply chain, reduced R&D,

Allows companies to attract new customers to their brand though an array of products that are similar but meet slightly different needs.

Customers as they can rely on their positive experience with an existing brand.

Adapt easily to market demand such as the iPhone 5SE (shows and example of market pull)

Role of the workforce

Training

The development of a highly skilled workforce can build deep understanding of how the production process works and allow workers at all levels to identify areas of the workflow to be improved.

This leads to the devolution of power

Devolution in power relating to process improvement

Understanding that the best people to identify improvements of a product or system are those who use it, companies striving for a lean production system ensure that all members of the workforce are able to contribute to the design of the system.

This benefits the company, which is able to streamline processes and reduce costs and also empowers the workforce and gives them a sense of ownership and loyalty to the company.

Kaizen

A philosophy and commitment to continuous process and product improvement

It is considered an important aspect of an organization's long-term strategy.

This has been central to the success of many Japanese companies such as Toyota.

It originated in Japan

Lead time

Lead time refers to the time quoted to customers (usually in days or weeks) between the date of purchase and the date of delivery.

It is basically the time frame it takes from the order of a product to its manufacture until it is delivery to the customer. This can be days or weeks in duration. This includes the production, set-up etc times.

The business dictionary has a bit more

The 5 Ss:

Sorting

Stabilizing

Shining

Standardizing

Sustaining the practice

5 'S'

A wikipedia reference to 5 'S'

The 7 wastes:

7 Wastes

Overproduction

Waiting

Transporting

Inappropriate processing

Unnecessary inventory

Unnecessary/excess motion

Defects.

Theory of Knowledge

The importance of the individual is recognized in design processes. Is this the case in other areas of knowledge?

International mindedness

The implementation of lean production has benefits for the global environment.

10.3 COMPUTER INTEGRATED MANUFACTURING

When considering design for manufacture (DfM), designers should be able to integrate computers from the earliest stage of design. This requires knowledge and experience of the manufacturing processes available to ensure integration is efficient and effective. Through the integration of computers, the rate of production can be increased and errors in manufacturing can be reduced or eliminated, although the main advantage is the ability to create automated manufacturing processes.

The integration of computer control into manufacturing can streamline systems, negating the need for time-consuming activities, such as stocktaking, but also reducing the size of the workforce.

CIM

A system of manufacturing that uses computers to integrate the processing of production, business and manufacturing in order to create more efficient production lines.

Programmable computer based manufacturing system

Typically, it relies on closed-loop control processes, based on real-time input from sensors

Wikipedia reference

Elements of CIM:

Design (CAD) – the product is designed within the CAD software, tested and the necessary G-Code, materials, and other data is generated.

Planning – the computer system and database (contains design and production data) helps to plan the most efficient production process.

Purchasing – with the design and production the computer system can employ a JIT approach in purchasing the necessary materials.

Cost accounting – is the budgeting of the production process, receipts, and all things financial.

Inventory control – responsible for tracking the materials, products, again JIT can be employed.

Distribution – is receiving materials and the distribution of products to warehouse or vendors.

CIM and scales of production

It is costly to set up

Therefore it is better suited for large scale production such as batch, volume or mass

Advantages and disadvantages of CIM in relation to different production systems

Scale of ProductionAdvantageDisadvantage

One – off or small scale

Costs are too to high to be used therefore not suited

Not suited for non-complex products

Batch, Volume or Mass

Nicely suited for batch due to the high flexibility and automation of CIM systems

Suited for volume and mass due to the fully automated nature of CIM

Monitoring of system at all times

Great machine utilisation

Fewer errors and waste

Improvements in productivity and quality control

Greater consistency

Cheaper products

Parts easily manufactured and changed

Random introduction of parts

Less lead time

Less labor

Higher quality of finish

High initial investment and personnel,

Training cost

Job losses

Lack of individuality

Mass Customisation

More choice,

Can design in own requirements

cheaper products

Parts easily manufactured and changed

Random introduction of parts

Less lead time

Higher quality of finish

High initial investment and personnel,

Training cost

Job losses

Advantages and disadvantages of CIM in relation to initial investment and maintenance

Advantages:

System is constantly monitored so if there is a breakdown: the type and location of breakdown is easily identified making maintenance easier

reduces cost of maintenance

After the high initial greater profits will be achieved

Disadvantage:

high initial capital costs/investments due to computers, robots, training of personnel

maintenance is complex, requires highly skilled employees

International Mindedness

A CIM system allows for efficient global workflow and distribution.

Theory of Knowledge

Technology has a profound influence in design. How have other areas of knowledge been influenced by technology?

10.4 QUALITY MANAGEMENT

Designers should ensure that the quality of products

is consistent through development of detailed manufacturing requirements. They also need to focus on the means to achieve it. The importance of quality management through quality control (QC), statistical process control (SPC) and quality assurance (QA) reduces the potential waste of resources.

The implementation of quality management strategies requires a critical and complete understanding of the needs of a product. To ensure efficiency and efficacy, these measures need to be designed into the product and its production system.

QC, SPC and QA are important aspects that contribute to quality management.

Be sure to identify the differences between QC, SPC and QA .

Quality control (QC)

Tolerances are defined at the design stage of the machinery. Parts not within tolerance need to be reworked or scrapped.

Continuous monitoring ensures that the machines perform to the pre-determined standard/quality.

Ensures that process inputs, such as speed, temperature, pressure, etc, are monitored an adjusted.

Quality control at the source eliminates waste from defects as workers are responsible for the quality of the work they do.

Able to get the same results over time

Quality assurance (QA)

This covers all activities from design to documentation.

It also includes the regulation of the quality of raw materials, assemblies, products and components, services related to production, and management and inspection processes.

It is the maintenance of the entire system from design to purchasing to packaging that meets quality requirements.

QAProcess orientatedPro-activePrevent defects

QCProduct orientatedReactiveFind defects

Statistical process control (SPC)

This is a quality control tool that uses statistical methods to ensure that a process operates at its most efficient.

This is achieved through measuring aspects of a component to ensure that it meets the required standard throughout its production in order to eliminate waste.

International Mindedness

Effective quality management can have major benefits for the environment.

Theory of Knowledge

There are commonly accepted ways of assuring quality in design. How do other areas of knowledge ensure the quality of their outputs?

10.5 ECONOMIC VIABILITY

Designers need to consider how the costs of materials, manufacturing processes, scale of production and labour contribute to the retail cost of a product. Strategies for minimizing these costs at the design stage are most effective to ensure that a product is affordable and can gain a financial return.

The economic viability of a product is paramount for designers if they are to get their product into production. Understanding how to design a product to specification, at lowest cost and to the appropriate quality while giving added value, can determine the relationship between what a product is worth and how much it costs.

Cost-effectiveness

The most efficient way of designing and producing a product from the manufacturer's point of view.

Costs that the manufacture is likely to incur, such as, capital costs (machinery and factory), R&D, Marketing, energy, overheads, taxes, profits, storage etc

Value for money

The relationship between what something, for example a product, is worth and the cash amount spent on it

The consumer decides if it was well worth spending the money on something.

It is an individual judgement and different people will value something differently.

Costing versus pricing:

In production, research, retail, and accounting, a cost is the value of money that has been used up to produce something.

Pricing is the process of determining what a company will receive in exchange for its product or service. The potential profit.

More examples include labour, manufacturing costs, costs relating to availability and procurement of materials, profits and taxes, size and weight of product for storage and distribution, resources, distribution and sales.

Fixed costs

The costs that must be paid out before production starts, for example, machinery. These costs do not change with the level of production.

Fixed costs, indirect costs or overheads are business expenses that are not dependent on the level of goods or services produced by the business, i.e., not reliant on output.

More examples include, scale of production, complexity of product, skills, quality control, type of advertising and marketing, R&D, capital costs, overheads, labour (directly related to production output).

Variable costs

Variable costs are costs that change in proportion to the goods or service that a business produces, i.e. reliant on output.

These costs are incurred once production starts.

These include, materials (processed and raw), utilities (electricity, water etc), wages, storage, distribution.

Fixed costs and variable costs make up the two components of total cost.

Costs

Cost analysis

It is a tool used to determine the potential risks and gains of producing a product.

It is used by manufacturers to determine the break-even point for a product and can be used to create multiple scenarios for a product.

It allows the feasibility of a product to be established.

Break-even

It is the point of balance between profit and loss. It represents the number of sales of a product required to cover the total costs (fixed and variable).

The break-even level or break-even point (BEP) represents the sales amount—in either unit or revenue terms—that is required to cover total costs (both fixed and variable). Total profit at the break-even point is zero. Break-even is only possible if a firm's prices are higher than its variable costs per unit.

Break Even Point

Calculating Product Price

Designers must consider encomium feasibility of their designs.

When companies calculate the price of their products they use Pricing Strategies described below.

Often more than one strategy would be used.

The below strategies can be used in conjunction with the Price Setting Strategies listed in topic 9.3: Marketing mix.

Price Setting Strategies include: cost-plus pricing, demand pricing, competitor-based pricing, product line pricing, psychological pricing.

Pricing strategies:

Price-minus

The market demand determines the product pricing (selling price) before manufacturing begins.

Then all commercial costs (manufacture, profits, etc) are determined and the company works within these constraints.

Retail price

It is the recommended retail price (RRP) suggested by the manufacturer (MSRP) that the retailer should sell the product for.

It is to standardise prices

Some retailers will sell below the RRP to lure customers.

Wholesale price

The cost of a product sold by the wholesaler.

The product costs more than the manufacturer but less than the retailer.

Typical manufacturing price

It is the total costs (variable and fixed) to manufacture the product. Divide the total manufacturing/product costs by the total products/items produced to get the average cost/price per unit.

Once total costs are determined then a profit margin is added.

The goal is to maximise profit.

Target cost

It is desired final cost of a product is determined before manufacturing begins.

This is based on the competing pricing.

Profit is then removed to determine initial cost.

The product is design or designed to meet it

Wikipedia on target costing

Return on investment (ROI)

Receiving a profit (return) on money invested into the product or service.

Usually expressed as a percentage.

The higher the ROI the better return

Unit cost

The costs a company incurs to produce store and sell one product (item).

This is calculated as an average cost.

These include fixed and variable costs

Sales volume

It is the amount of products sold in a specified time period during regular working operations of a company.

They can be annual, quarterly, etc sales

Can also be based on demographics, geographic regions, etc

Financial return

It is the profits generated from a sale or investment into a company.

Activity: Calculation of prices based on the listed pricing strategies.

International Mindedness

The cost effectiveness of a product can determine whether it can enter economically diverse national and international markets.

Theory of Knowledge

The retail price of a product is partly based on evidence of its potential position in the market. What counts as evidence in various areas of knowledge?

Work Cited:

http://en.wikipedia.org/wiki/Break-even_(economics)
http://en.wikipedia.org/wiki/Fixed_cost
http://en.wikipedia.org/wiki/Variable_cost
http://en.wikipedia.org/wiki/Cost%E2%80%93benefit_analysis

www.ingramcontent.com/pod-product-compliance
Lightning Source LLC
Chambersburg PA
CBHW080905160726
48000CB00009B/2865